WHAT WILL HAPPEN TO
MY SPECIAL NEEDS CHILD
WHEN I AM GONE?

A Detailed Guide To Secure Your Child's Emotional And Financial Future

– Susan Jules

Thank you for buying this Different Not Less e-book.

To receive special offers, bonus content, and info on new releases and other great reads, sign up for our newsletters.

Visit us online at

www.differentnotless.us

The author and publisher have provided this e-book to you for your personal use only. You may not make this e-book publicly available in any way. Copyright infringement is against the law. If you believe the copy of this e-book you are reading infringes on the author's copyright, please notify us at https://differentnotless.us/pages/piracy.

*To Nathan for Everything.
You are my Life!*

Table of Contents

Chapter 1	Introduction	1
Chapter 2	Prevailing Family and Societal Challenges	13
Chapter 3	What the Law Says	29
Chapter 4	Broaching the Subject of Mortality with Our Child(ren)	41
Chapter 5	Broaching the Subject of Mortality with Your Child(ren) Continued	51
Chapter 6	Managing Grief	63
Chapter 7	The Uphill Task of Single Parenting	72
Chapter 8	While You Are Here	80
Chapter 9	The Right Education	92
Chapter 10	The Right Health Care	105
Chapter 11	The Right Support	115
Chapter 12	Development Assessment and Journaling	121
Chapter 13	Before You Leave	128
Chapter 14	Fundamentals of Crafting a Will	140
Chapter 15	Letter of Intent and Care Plan	150
Chapter 16	Special Needs Trust, Life Insurance	159
Chapter 17	Estate Planning - Quick Summary	172
Chapter 18	When You Are Gone	178
Chapter 19	Guardianship	191

Chapter 20	Your Child with Special Needs and Their Workplace	198
Chapter 21	Your Child's Involvement in Your Funeral Plans	204
Chapter 22	Securing Continued Growth and Development	211
	Conclusion	227

Chapter 1
Introduction

The Challenges Involved In Raising Children with Special Needs in an Unfriendly World

The topic of parenting has undoubtedly garnered a lot of attention over the years. One of the biggest challenges in this sphere centers on parenting a child/children with special needs. This is no simple role at all, which is why many families struggle with the commensurate challenges that accompany the process of parenting children with special needs.

These challenges, whether natural or made-made, can be the defining factor that brings happiness for parents, their children with special needs, or their utter misery. And over the years, these same challenges have led to a handful of discouraged parents and children alike, huge struggles for affected families to lead normal lives, and the inability of society to homogenously integrate them effectively, amongst many other unpleasant results.

Amongst these many challenges, which we will look closely at later, is the challenge of parents securing the best care and future for the lives of their children with special needs in an event where they are no longer available to do so themselves. It is unimaginable for most parents to think of what the life of their wards would be like when they are no longer alive. For the parents of children with special needs, there is often a nagging belief that their wards would be left helpless in a world filled with so much chaos, with nothing or no one to turn to.

Looking at the efforts that governments of nations around the world have and are putting in place, all geared at providing care and protection for children with special needs, there is so much to be desired. Granted, a handful of nations have taken deliberate steps to ensure that parents who are responsible for children with special needs receive some kinds of benefits in terms of education grants, tax relief, social amenities, and the like; still others, through the instrument of legislation, have gone further to enact laws that serve to recognize, emphasize, and protect the rights of children with special needs, some examples being the United States of America's Individuals with Disabilities Education Act (IDEA), 2004 and the United Kingdom's Children and Families Act, 2014. But taking a quick glance at the broad spectrum, one would notice that these efforts do not cut evenly across the board and are barely enough to effectively offer the much-needed cover they require. With some countries having little or no laws enacted in this regard and doing nothing in particular to support either the parents or the primary caregiver of children with special needs residing with them, it paints a very bleak picture with respect to the future of these children.

It is a fact that parents/guardians are keen on affording the best for their child/ward with special needs. According to the statistics gotten from the MetLife's survey titled *2005 The Torn Security Blanket: Children with Special Needs and the*

Planning Gap, and *the 2011 Torn Security Blanket Study*[1], about 69 percent of families admit growing and serious concerns about their abilities to afford lifetime support for their wards with special needs, and these concerns extend to the boundaries of thoughts of what would become of their wards when they die.

Furthermore, 88 percent of parents catering to children with special needs have not at any time established any form of trust aimed at preserving eligibility for their child with special needs when it comes to essential benefits such as Medicaid and complementary social income; in the last two decades, on the other hand, there has been a noticeable spike in the number of special needs trusts established by various caregivers, growing by an impressive 21 percent, effectively doubling the figures recorded back in 2005.

Again, figures indicating the number of caregivers who have neither written nor signed a letter of intent delineating an arrangement for the future care of the child with special needs stayed at 84 percent, with 72 percent not designating or naming any trustee to manage their child's estate in the event of the parents' passing. Furthermore, 56 percent admitted their ignorance on the subject and wherewithal of identifying and naming a trustee to look over the financial holdings of their dependent in the future.

While two decades ago, only 53 percent had not named a guardian for their child, the number has slightly improved today to 49 percent. Still, about 59 percent of caregivers admit that they have little or no information about the financial assistance at their disposal, either on the subject of benefits and support delivered by state agencies or on legal steps for securing the future of their wards; in fact, 55 percent believe that this information is extremely hard to find.

Further surveys also revealed that 33 percent of parents spend time, which could be equated to a full-time job, taking care of their child with special needs; about forty hours per week on an average. Coupled with such an enormous amount of hours is the fact that these parents of children with special needs typically spend $326 per month, which amounts to about $4000 per year on unbudgeted medical expenditures to cater for their child with special needs.

Finally, it was also noted that 38 percent of caregivers have penned down a will, which is quite good compared to two decades ago, when the figures only stood at 32 percent. And for those who went further to set up future housing plans for their wards, the numbers stood at 36 percent, going up from 31 percent two decades ago.

These statistics clearly indicate that while some level of progress has been made in the last couple of years, there needs to be concerted effort between various governmental and social stakeholders in securing the future of children with special needs.

(a) Children with Special Needs

A child with special needs is an adolescent that has been understood to have a need for special devotion and specific requirements that other children do not need. Typically, such a status is declared by the state with the singular resolve of proposing benefits and support for the child's general growth and development. The term "Special needs" can likewise carry a legal connotation or designation, principally in the fostering and adoption care community. Here, the parent, caregiver, or guardian gets provisions geared at supporting them in leading dynamic lives.

By sheer definition and covering the subject of diagnostics, special needs is a blanket term. Its scope can stretch to a range which captures challenges that may last for life, others that may be comparatively mild, and those that are best described as profound. It captures within it medical challenges, developmental delays, psychiatric disorders, and hereditary illnesses that necessitate continuous support so that the child with special needs can attain their best potential.

Notable Points

- *The characterization of special needs in reference to a child takes account of an extensive multiplicity of conditions, which may include corporal infirmities, learning disabilities, and life-threatening diseases.*
- *Parents and primary caregivers of children with special needs typically get some form of supplementary tax credit or deduction to help offset the added expenses and struggles that accompany giving care to children with special needs.*
- *A number of children with special needs do well in public schools that propose a wide variety of scholastic and emotional care programs, such as work-related therapy and one-on-one teacher assistance.*

(b) Classification of Children with Special Needs

IDEA was officially signed into law in 2004. It essentially guarantees that any child with special needs living in the United States of America will obtain services in the area of special education. Therein are four major types of children with special needs. These four types are further broken down into other thirteen classifications of uniqueness well defined under the Disabilities Education Act. So, for students to get special education, they would have to be clearly identified under at least one of the aforementioned classifications and particularly be in need of special education and support services.

Generally speaking, a typical case could be considered under the special needs category if an individual would need assistance in the following areas:
- Movement and motion
- Communication and interaction
- Decision-making and intelligence
- Self-care and independence

The six major types are listed as follows:

(i) Medical or physical needs: Medical or physical challenges for children may consist of severe bodily illnesses such as various forms of cancers, heart diseases, muscular dystrophy, cystic fibrosis, and the like. Other forms of illnesses also include protracted ailments such as diabetes, respiratory diseases, hereditary disorders such as dwarfism and cerebral palsy, and health challenges such as obesity and food sensitivities. This would typically require that the child gets recurrent medical diagnoses, admissions into hospital, and housing and equipment for incapacities. When handling such worries and any medical crises, for that matter, the formation of a robust support system is critically essential.

(ii) Developmental needs: Developmental frailties can dramatically alter the way a parent views the future; these can also be responsible for varying degrees of complications associated with effectively caring for and educating the child with special needs. Diseases such as Down syndrome, autism, and intellectual incapacities time and again give reasons for pulling children from the conventional educational facilities. In most cases, parents and caregivers become stern campaigners for the right kinds of services, education, therapy, and inclusion to be offered to their wards.

(iii) Behavioral/emotional needs: Children with behavior problems may not react positively to conventional discipline

as they ought to or as their peers do. Diseases such as fetal alcohol spectrum disorder, Tourette's syndrome, attention-deficit hyperactivity disorder, and dysfunctions of sensory integration often have a need for dedicated approaches that are custom-made to meet their unambiguous needs. Behavior disorders can further heighten the danger of encountering problems in the place of learning.

(iv) Education/learning needs: Irrespective of their intellectual aptitudes, children with learning frailties, such as auditory processing disorder and dyslexia, find it hard to cope with schoolwork. They have a need for dedicated education tactics carefully tailored to meet their potential, while avoiding injuring their self-esteem and encountering behavioral complications. It is worth mentioning that one of the key factors in raising kids with learning challenges is persistence. This means engaging your ward at every given opportunity to ensure they get all the help they need.

(v) Sensory impaired needs: These are children with special needs who have ailments or challenges associated with the effective use or function of their sensory organs. So they may have trouble interacting with their environment and illnesses such as blindness or various forms of visual impairments, deafness or various forms of limited hearing, speech and language impairments, and so on.

(vi) Mental health needs: Certain mental challenges such as anxiety, depression, or attachment difficulties can take serious tolls on a parent. These conditions differ from child to child, but have various similarities. Parents will deal with an upheaval of mood swings, predicaments, and defiance. Tailored professionalism is required for these; also, you will need to quickly embrace therapy, medications, and, in some cases, hospitalization.

(c) Pros and Cons of Special Needs Designation

There have been mixed reactions when it comes to the subject of labeling children with special needs, either using terminological or environmental designations. However, being labeled as a child with special needs has its fair share of pros and cons. Here are a few to consider.

(i) Pros:

1. *Carefully tailored education plan:* By accurately labeling a child who has special needs in the classroom, the chances of using this information as a guide to craft out an accurate education plan aimed at helping the child learn is greatly heightened. Experts say once a student is recognized as having special needs, the student can then be given an individualized education program (IEP) premeditated to cater for their distinctive needs. Accurately classifying students in particular categories of disability gives room for specialists to craft out an education plan precisely for the student, thereby meeting their educational needs.

2. *Additional support for learning:* By labeling children with special needs in the most accurate way possible, we put them in a pivotal position to take delivery of added services that they might not have hitherto been able to access otherwise. For instance, learning at a pace that may be convenient for the child can only be administered when they are identified and placed within such an environment of learning. Certain teaching techniques, such as frequent repetition and slow-paced instructions, can be effected in a much smaller setting, alongside other students of the same classification.

3. *Tailored tutoring:* Once a child is accurately identified as having a learning disability, then the solutions and remedies being channeled toward their development would be properly fine-tuned. So by receiving instructions that were carefully formulated to meet the student's peculiar need, they are most likely to excel and develop better. Additionally, by adequate identification, the teachers are better placed to tutor the child with special needs in a fashion that makes certain that the child learns, indeed. This they do by employing specific learning tools and skill set meant for students with special needs.

(ii) Cons:

1. *Tendency for the student to develop low self-esteem:* Inasmuch as laws have been enacted to safeguard the rights of students with special needs, as well as access to services, serving to make sure these students are not victimized, research has shown that labeling can negatively impact the self-esteem of children with special needs. Experts postulate that children who are labeled as special needs students may doubt themselves and develop learning helplessness through the feeling of not being smart enough or as compared to their counterparts. The impact could result in even worse results as the child might stop performing well in school, thereby affecting their general development.

2. *Parents' and teachers' diminished expectations for their wards:* A recent survey has indicated that 68 percent of people have a below par expectation set on children labeled as special needs children. Even more are parents, primary caregiver, caregivers, and teachers who unconsciously nurse soft spots toward their wards, which contributes significantly in lowering their expectations for their children with special needs. This might stem from a false belief that the student cannot do what is mandated of the other students. If care isn't taken, the child with special needs will begin to falter in reaching set academic goals. In all this, a chain of

consequence must be noted; if the teacher or parent doesn't have confidence in the child, then it wouldn't be out of place to infer that the child won't have confidence in himself/herself either. To step down one's expectations of a child with special needs is to set up the student for failure in the future.

3. *Challenges with peers:* Statistically, children with special needs are twice as likely to be bullied as their contemporaries. And sadly, thanks to labeling, this number could rise significantly. Schools do have pockets of students who can be unusually mean; they make fun of the student with special needs on occasion, simply because the former are different. This may amount to too much exposure for these children with special needs, crippling their opportunity to make new friends, ultimately making them vulnerable to bullying. It is imperative that these children, leaning upon the assistance of their teachers and parents, form positive self-images and improve their self-esteem. This their teachers and parents can do by aiding them in building strong relationships with others.

So getting parents adequately informed and actively involved in the formation and administration of the academic process of the child with special needs can help ensure that the good points of labeling significantly outweigh the points of concern. But regardless of the intention, this clearly spelt out description is expedient. This is because, with this, affected parents, caregivers, and primary caregivers can acquire the much-needed services they require, set apposite objectives, and gain requisite knowledge of their affected wards and the impending challenges they are bound to encounter as a family. Typically, the parent, caregiver, or guardian of the child with special needs would get some form of supplementary tax credit or deduction to help offset the added expenses and struggles that accompany giving care to children with special needs.

(c) Special Considerations for Children with Special Needs

The challenges parents and caregivers of children with special needs face are numerous; this implies that the former must be given some degree of peculiar consideration in any given society if they are to continue supporting the latter.

These medical and therapeutic considerations needed to uplift the quality of life for a majority of children with special needs, typically comes at great costs. How much the child has been ravaged by the prevailing condition(s) may demand extensive medical care to help attain a flourishing life for the child; a clear instance would be a child that is suffering from a terminal or body-deteriorating disease. There may be a need for regular monitoring in an event that the condition worsens over time. Equipment for support may be employed to arrange for the child's mobility in and around the home or place of learning; and in some cases, support animals such as specially trained dogs may be procured in a bid to pursue the best path toward total restoration.

Furthermore, a child designated as having special needs may need unconventional methods to foster their education; these methods usually would take into consideration their unique conditions, while delivering other creative ways for them to explore, thereby deepening their capacity to absorb and develop. A clear instance would be a child with diminished corporal mobility or with challenges in interacting via conventional vocal cues.

In the aforementioned case, other unique methods would need to be adopted in teaching the child, while they are encouraged to apply those taught skills in the home or place of learning.

Again, the need to call on experts may arise when dealing with children with cognitive impairments. Such experts would explore ways of establishing and maintaining connections with such children with special needs. And with time, they can ensure that the children fully grasp vital lessons before recommending moving them to another stage of learning. All these come at exuberant costs and must be considered if a better life must be given to children with special needs.

Notable Points:
   (i) *IDEA was officially enacted into law in 2004.*
   (ii) *Tailored definitions and descriptions do abound. However, a case must fall under one or more of these characteristics before it can be so designated: impairments in movement and motion, communication and interaction, decision-making and intelligence, and self-care and independence.*
   (iii) *The designation of children with special needs helps in achieving tailored learning, garnering added support and tutelage.*
   (iv) *Such a designation, however, can lead to the formation of low self-esteem in the child, diminished expectations from others, and challenges of interactions with peers.*
   (v) *Children would always require special considerations, while their parents or caregivers work twice as hard as their contemporaries to give them a better life.*

Actionable Steps:
   (i) *Take a pen and paper and write down what you know about IDEA.*
   (ii) *Take out time to research further on the provisions in the IDEA.*
   (iii) *What are your thoughts about the designation of children with special needs?*

Write down some of the considerations that you think your child with special needs should be given.

Chapter 2
Prevailing Family and Societal Challenges

(a) What Many Parents Experience?

In many cases, a big part of the overall definitions and descriptions of special needs are generally hinged on what a child *cannot* do; inability to reach set goals, foods not to be ingested, activities never to be engaged in, practices never to be enjoyed, and so on. All of these restrictions can strike a family hard, making "special needs" appear to be a catastrophic designation.

Granted, some parents will at regular times mourn the lost potentials of their child, and might in fact see their ward's condition simply become worse as time passes. Still for others, they may find pleasant triumphs in the challenges before them, pushing them to walk in strength even in moments of weakness.

As regards the challenges of raising children with special needs, there are no two families that are the same, even though they both might share a few things in common. For instance, a family managing challenges in the area of developmental delays will have concerns that are poles apart from another family managing challenges in the area of terminal ailments. The same applies for other families dealing with anxieties, mental disorders, erudition, or behavioral challenges.

The common challenges of parenting are further compounded for parents and primary caregivers of children with special needs, thanks to the numerous huddles they get to encounter on a daily basis. A few challenges include having to extensively learn about the disability of their wards, carrying out researches which cover accessing treatments and resources, dealing with the demands (both emotional and physical) of nurturing an individual with a disability, and meeting numerous appointments with health care providers, therapists, campaigners, and educationists. It also includes advocating for mediations, accommodations, placements, and disbursing payments for the numerous treatments and interventions not captured by health insurance. These and more are consistently at the feet of parents and primary caregivers.

(i) *Stress:* Stress is one challenge that parents of those with special needs face regularly. New research has indicated that moms of adolescents and adults living with autism have stress hormones at the same levels with soldiers in active combat. There are a number of reasons for such high levels of stress, one of which is finances. Typically, in a quest to effect suitable care, one of the parents, usually the mother takes a break from her job or career just so that she can focus on the child with special needs. The result, however, ends up negatively impacting huge financial losses for the family, thereby compounding stress.

(ii) *Anxiety and worry:* Parents of children with special needs have a tendency to drift into excessive fears: fears over the agony and suffering being experienced by their wards and the likelihood of it escalating, fears over their future, whether or not they would ever recover, and the question of whether they as parents are giving an adequate amount of their resources and energy, doing right by their child.

(iii) *Grief and anguish:* Primary caregivers or parents can feel their hopes and aspirations for their child(ren) being dashed, especially if the illnesses are intensifying. Also, they may feel anguish once they are convinced that they do not have the parenting experience required to efficiently cater for a child with special needs. Furthermore, once they are reminded of what their wards are missing out on, it can cause a resurgence of grief.

(iv) *Guiltiness and remorse:* Guilt can be a huge challenge for a family responsible for a child with special needs. Their limitations as caregivers to protect the child can weigh in on them from time to time. Also, the loss of attention toward other children might creep in, leaving wounds that might take time and energy to heal; such negligence by one or both parents can ruin other vital relationships with their fellow spouse, friends, relatives, or even aged parents. Furthermore, such feelings can come up when parents see other children whom they might best describe as "normal." The feeling of jealousy and resentment could take over and do extensive damage if care is not taken.

(v) *Feelings of isolation:* The task of taking care of a child with special needs can cause an entire family to go into isolation. First, it could happen because they cannot get their ward to actively engage in any social activities with other families; so they are forced to sit out many family-oriented activities. Again, to avoid pointless criticisms and judgments from people who know little or nothing about the condition of the child with special needs, the parents embrace isolation as a way out. Furthermore, the odd feeling of being perceived as an outsider amongst other parents who do not have this unique challenge can further drive families away from social interactions.

(vi) *Self-care and sustenance:* Statistically, parents of children with special needs are every so often fatigued and often become depressed. Their time and resources are often depleted, even more depleted than parents of unaffected children. Nevertheless, they possess a deep desire and need for refueling. The needs of parents must be carefully factored in as an important element in the entire process of nurturing the child with special needs.

Surprisingly, the most helpful support parents get is from other parents of children with similar special needs. There are a lot of peer support networks founded by various organizations and advocacy groups, which help to provide a link between families who share the same challenges. Mutual discussions and sharing of stories can help strengthen parents as they may share stories, resources, and advice that assist one another.

(b) *Exiting Without Adequate Preparation*

Patrick and Susan Swallow (not their real names) were dedicated parents to their adolescent son Daren, who was officially categorized as a child with special needs since the age of two. Together, they invested quite a lot of resources and effort in managing their son's condition of autism. Tragedy struck when Patrick passed away; Daren was only nine at the time. So after coping with the loss of her husband, Susan went on to give her best to her son. Now, Susan is worried; she woke up one morning to the rather devastating thought, "What would happen to Daren if, like his father, I unexpectedly die?"

Martin Stoley (not his real name) has been in therapy for the past month. He has been getting help for a number of psychological challenges he has been dealing with. His daughter Miranda, a twelve-year-old child with learning disabilities, has been his pillar of strength through his trying times. But, thanks to the many sacrifices he had to make to meet his therapeutic commitments, he and his daughter have had to endure small periods apart for the very first time since she was born. It was during one of those periods of brief separation that Martin began to realize how unprepared he was about leaving his daughter for any reason. Soon, he had to face the tough question of how his daughter would cope in the event of his demise.

Like Susan and Martin, there are many parents and caregivers of children with special needs who are completely unprepared to leave their wards; for many, it is unthinkable and even forbidden to mention. But the reality remains; there would come a time when you, as a loving parent, will be permanently separated from your child with special needs. This means you would no longer have a say on how your ward's life would be run or maintained.

Recent surveys indicate that amongst children and young people, those with disabilities or those who have special needs are more likely to dwell in perpetual poverty compared to their counterparts without a disability. However, pupils identified with special educational needs (SEN) were found to be more likely to be qualified (about 27.5 percent) for free school meals compared to their counterparts without SEN.

Furthermore, taking care of a child with special needs has been proven to be costly. About 33 percent of families who were responsible for taking care of a child with special needs has reported an increase in expenditure of over $300 every month or total costs up to $80,000 from birth to age eighteen. From this number, only about 56 percent of these families have this increment partly covered thanks to their disability benefits.

Unpreparedness for such an occurrence can be dangerous as the world remains a brutal place to leave such an already vulnerable child to navigate on their own. There is no need to bury your head in the sand like an ostrich would; the sooner you ask and answer such hard questions, the better for your peace of mind and the future of your child with special needs.

(c) Dying Without a Will

It can be extremely challenging for estate administrators to manage cases where a person dies without a will. Even in the last thirty years, these seasoned professionals have been encouraging families to prepare a will before passing (with all the right reasons).

- Penning down a will is one of the surest means of leaving a lifelong heritage for your family in general and your child with special needs in particular, going on to financially secure their future in no small measure. After carrying out a good number of surveys on the subjects, experts were able to determine that such facts about writing down a will are extensively well known. However, for many reasons, a lot of people end up passing on without making it to an attorney's office to write down their last will. Below are a few statistics that show how unprepared many people around the world are for the inevitable. A survey carried out in 2012 indicated that 71 percent of adults living in America between the age brackets of twenty-five to thirty-four did not possess a legal will. And even more shocking was the fact that 45 percent of parents, those who ought to have already written theirs, did not have a will either. Another survey carried out in the United Kingdom, indicated that a stunning 75 percent of individuals who had hitherto already written their will had not reviewed it in the past decade, even when, for most of the surveyed individuals, their lives had undergone remarkable changes in their relationships, financial worth, and businesses spanning the same period.

- In 2013, reports of a survey carried out in the United Kingdom by two major independent online outfits indicated that 58 percent of the adult population have not written down their will. And while the number of under-forty UK residents who had no will stood at 69 percent, older adults/individuals between the ages of forty and fifty who had not written down their last will stood at 54 percent.
- Another survey indicated the weird fact that only about 67 percent of people are aware of the actual place where the original copies of their parents' will can be accessed.
- While 25 percent of young adults living in the UK are completely ignorant of how to go about writing a will, let alone owning one at the time; another 23 percent

indicated that they hadn't considered writing down a will, owing to the fact that they were rather poor and therefore had nothing to will to anyone.
- Further surveys indicate that the people most likely to be immensely affected by adults not writing down their last will before passing on are their children. Statistically, about 77 percent of parents residing within the UK who have no more than five children have indicated that they do not yet have a written will.
- A study in Australia by an independent online outfit indicated that 50 percent of adults residing in that nation did not have a written will.
- In 2014, a Law Society article published that the government of the United Kingdom took possession of a massive £8 million worth of property from individuals in 2013 alone. Those properties absorbed by the government belonged to people who had passed on without leaving a will.

All the aforementioned information helps to establish a clear picture, which is that a lot of the people who ought to have already written their will are yet to do so and, consequently, would end up passing on without ever doing so. In addition, the few that did write their will at one time or the other have failed to judiciously follow up and update the legal document as and when due.

The question then arises: Why don't a lot of people write their will despite being aware of the importance and the manifold complications that might come up in the event that they neglect it? Here are a few points to answer this question:
- For many young people, they hold a delusory outlook about death; most feel they are too young to die. Therefore, they see no need to prepare for it as they still

have more time at their disposal to do so. Surprisingly, this notion is held by even older adults in some instances. This leads them to further procrastinate, which eventually ends up in them never writing a will.
- For most people, writing a will is an activity reserved strictly for the wealthy. After all, why write a will when there is nothing to will out to anyone?
- Another reason why most people do not bother writing their will is that most think it comes at a steep price. Also, others think it is ridiculously time-consuming, being too long a process to endure and not worth the stress.
- For some, writing a will is tantamount to acknowledging the reality of one's frailty before death. In fact, some think by doing so, one opens their mind to the thought and possibility of dying in the near future.
- Some feel what they possess can be amicably distributed amongst their family members without necessarily birthing any quarrel among them. They simply do not see the sharing of their estate as a possible bone of contention.
- Some simply feel they don't have the wherewithal to go about writing a will; for them, learning how to go about it is needless as their minds already see it as something that is beyond them.
- Some think of their affairs as too complicated, too technical to be captured in a will to the utmost detail. For these kinds of people, they would rather sit it out than complicate things further.
- Some express great reservation in opening up the details of their estate to an outsider—in this case, their lawyer. For one reason or the other, they fear that such revelations would be used against them in the future.

- Some think writing a will is needless as their financial, economic, and social conditions are constantly changing. They feel going to update their will frequently would constitute a nuisance to their lives.
- Some find selecting an executor for their will extremely challenging; others have a hard time making up their minds about who would be the guardian of their kids, the manager of their businesses and assets. This has slowed them down on the issue of writing a last will.
- Some of these reasons may appear valid and completely reasonable, but not a single one of them is adequate justification for anyone not writing down a will. Once proper knowledge about the subject is deployed, a change of mindset is attained, and proper planning is carried out, one should be on the path to writing their last will.

(d) *A Few Points to Remember about Writing a Will*

Take the steps to write your will immediately. No matter how much thought you have given to the exercise before now, nothing beats writing a will now. Regardless of what age bracket you fall under, the fact remains that there is no absolute certainty that you will live as long as you expect. Again, it does not matter what amount of possession you have; it is still imperative that the little you have, be shared in a manner that you desire when you pass on.

Frequently review your will. After you have drafted your will, it is important that you return to it from time to time for an update. Updating it is important as your life must have changed since the last time you wrote it. So visit your will at least once every year, so that you can make modifications to show fresh ups and downs in your family, business, and other things that are dear to you. Keeping an out-of-date will can be as obsolete as not having one in the first place. *Inform others about the existence of your will.* Having a will that is exclusively known to you alone is a disaster waiting to happen. In fact, such an action is in no way dissimilar from not possessing a will in the first place. This is because the resulting concerns are the same. To realize your aim for writing a will, there is a need to inform your loved ones of such a development. Tell them that you have written one, where you have it held in reserve, and how they can repossess it when you pass away.

So what happens when a person dies without writing a last will? The first thing is that the deceased is considered to have died *intestate.* This designation implies that all the properties belonging to the deceased would be disseminated in accordance with the intestacy statute of the state in question. Inasmuch as state laws vary, they, by and large, arrange for such properties to be disseminated amongst the spouse and children of the decedent, if any, then to parents, if any. In cases where no one is available from those classes, the statutes will largely seek siblings, then grandparents, and other more distant relatives. This search would continue until an heir is found.

Such occurrences, especially in the demise of really wealthy people, tend to bring about the emergence of claims from various parties who would seek a claim on the estate.

It is for the most part essential for people with children having special needs to have a plan in place that takes into account special needs planning. Establishing a trust for a child with special needs allows you to provide for the child in a way that does not put at risk any government benefits to which the child might be eligible to as a result of their disability. While such a concern might not be a worry for well-to-do families, others who are more modest and whose assets cannot effectively provide the often excessive budget attendant with giving a lifetime of support to a child with special needs should seek legal guidance as soon as possible if they have not previously done so.

One of the vital things that would be conspicuously stated in a last will is the designation of the legal guardian(s) who would be responsible for any minor children, whether with special needs or not. But if a will isn't available, the court will choose who would cater to the children of the deceased; this choice would have absolutely no input from the deceased in any way.

The use of different types of trusts by parents or children with special needs can help not only make immediate provision for children with special needs but can also freeze any of their assets in a living trust. This would then be transferred outside of probate if ever they die. Establishing a trust is known to be a faster, inexpensive, and more cloistered way of transferring assets to any intended beneficiary. This is because trust assets pass outside of the public probate process. Also, there are a lot of tax benefits, alongside other reasons to integrate revocable and irrevocable trusts in one's estate plan.

Notable Points

(i) There are obvious challenges parents of children with special needs often experience, from coping with enormous stress, anxiety and grief, to outright isolation and a breakdown of personal health.

(ii) One of the most prominent challenges is dying without drafting a will.

(iii) With statistics supporting the fact that will drafting isn't common practice amongst most people, it nevertheless is important.

(iv) *The fears of the unknown, poverty, laziness, secrecy, and indifference are some of the reasons why many do not yet have written wills.*

(v) *It is imperative that you write your will immediately, review it as often as you can, and inform loved ones about how to access it when you are gone.*

(e) The Downside of Unpreparedness

So what are the possibilities that exist as far as exiting the world without making adequate preparation for a child with special needs is concerned? Here are a few points to contemplate:

- An unprepared exit could mean that there would be no occasion for the parent to choose a guardian(s) fit for any minor they might have, particularly caregivers for their child(ren) with special needs. In the event that this happens, it then implies that the government would, without doubt, become the public guardian of the bereaved ward. For most people, leaving their child with special needs in the custody of the government is unacceptable as they don't think their child would get the best care they require from a public guardian. This is a valid concern, and it makes it expedient for every parent to be deliberate with this decision before the time comes. It goes without question that any parent can relate to how imperative it is to ensure that their child is in the hands of a trusted guardian once they are dead.

- Exiting without a will, for instance, would mean there would be no executor to anything and everything you leave behind. Now, this occurrence could be completely unpleasant for your child with special needs, and, thus, should be avoided. There are cases of outright abandonment of the bereaved children and the misappropriation of their inheritances by swindlers who stand in as friends or relatives, for the sake of there not being any legally designated executor. Apart from the possibility of your ward being left in the hands of rogues, the absence of such a key figure could breed many other complications in the dividend and disbursement of your estate; issues such as delays, needless expenses, outright frustrations, and in some cases, loss can occur.

- No matter what plans parents have for their children with special needs—the desire to open a trust in their name, the plan to set aside some funds for their education or medical bills, or the desire to hand them some money when they reach maturity—all these cannot be actualized if plans are not made in time before the eventual exit of the parents. If any of such plans aren't properly made and taken care of using the various instruments and channels, then such children run the risk of entering childhood without having to experience all their parents desired, for which arrangements were never made. Furthermore, an unprepared exit could mean wards that cannot fend for themselves, upon reaching the legal age of maturity, would be forced to receive funds which they may not have the capacity to disburse/utilize them in ways that would benefit them.

- Another thing to consider is that in the case where the child is still a minor, if no preparation is made as regards their future, the government, after taking up the role of public guardian, would appoint a public trustee, who would oversee all affairs in the management of the child's share of the estate. By implication, the financial future of such a child with special needs would be solely decided by the government, one way or another. And as a fee, part of the estate would be relinquished to the government. Sadly, this sizably cuts down whatever was left off for the child.

- Life insurance has been used by many families as a method of injecting liquid funds into their estate. But in the case where parents don't take advantage of such opportunities, upon such a tragic exit like death, then some valuable assets that were left behind intended for keeps or further investment purposes would have to be sold off to make funds available for the many exigencies that might arise. This could be counterproductive to the future of the child.

- The fact remains that subjecting one's partner and child with special needs to the many ups and downs dealing with lawyers and courts can be very heartbreaking. Again, upon one's death, the ensuing legal battle would cost huge amounts in tax and legal fees; so that at the end, so much that could have gone toward the future of the child with special needs would be lost. Therefore, it would be wise to save money on taxes, lawyers, and court costs following your demise. Surprisingly, it takes far less in fees to set up a will than it would cost hiring a lawyer and paying various fees when a problem is encountered with an estate.

- Unpreparedness can come with bitter consequences, impacting directly on the child with special needs. In the case where an entire family passes away, leaving only the child with special needs who is still a minor, the estate may have to be held by a relative who may have no strong connection to the family or may even have had feuds with the family before the tragic incident occurred. Such could spell doom for the child. Therefore, it is

strongly advised that due diligence be paid in setting up a legacy via charitable gifting.
- In some states where there is no recognition of common law relationships or same-sex relationships under the Intestate Succession Act, it is expedient that certain steps be put in place to avoid the possibility of total forfeiture of one's estate after demise.
- In an event where parents leave behind a very large family, say plenty of children and grandchildren, one of the points of conflict and division is the unexpected exit of one or both parents without leaving behind adequate preparation of how their estate ought to be managed or shared. In the midst of all the conflicts, the hardest hit is usually the child with special needs. Most times, resolving such deep conflicts would require the liquidation of existing businesses and properties. With proper and timely planning, one is able to leave certain things aimed at protecting the future of the child with special needs. In fact, the testator might even decide to protect the future of the grandchildren. So, it is essential to plan to circumvent possible conflicts.

Actionable Steps

(i) *Take a pen and notebook and write out some of the challenges that you feel are unique to being a parent of a child special needs.*

(ii) *Have you at any point in the past ever written a will before?*

(iii) *Write down some of your fears concerning writing down a will.*

Write down your thoughts about dying without being prepared.

Chapter 3
What the Law Says

(a) *Legal and Illegal Issues Surrounding the Care for Children with Special Needs*

As stated earlier, many countries have done their bit in trying to help the child with special needs attain some level of comfort, exercise their fundamental human rights, and live normal lives without fear of discrimination, bullying, or intimidation. These efforts, even though not nearly enough, have so far helped to effectively shape society enough to wholesomely accommodate the child with special needs. But to be an actual activist for your child with special needs, you must first seek to understand the laws that are in effect, aimed at protecting your child with special needs.

Federal laws standardize special education services, ensuring that schools make accommodation available for children with disabilities. Additionally, antibullying laws have since been enacted by almost all states and are being fully implemented. So by having a firm mental grasp on these laws, along with full knowledge of the rights of your child, you would have empowered yourself to be able to defend your ward against partial or prejudiced treatment. Let us explore a few laws that affect children with disability and children with special needs.

(i) Individuals with Disabilities Education Act: The law was ratified sometime in 2004; the IDEA makes certain that all classified children with disabilities have the right of entry to an unrestricted and suitable public education. Details of the law spell out special education benefits, including personalized special education services. Typically, every state is unique when it comes to applying their laws; however, they all have to maintain consistency with the IDEA.

So schools must adhere to the following, in harmony with the six basic principles outlined in Part B of the IDEA:

- *The provision of free and suitable public education:* Schools are obligated to arrange for education at the expense of the public, which would be strictly under the supervision and direction of the public.
- *Carry out an effective evaluation assessment:* Schools are required to collect the necessary information that would assist in determining the educational needs of the child; furthermore, the school is required to make appropriate decisions about educational programming.
- *Produce an individualized education program:* In a bid to see how the individual needs of the child with special needs are tended to, schools are required to craft out a written statement that captures the educational program premeditated for the child.
- *Arrange for a less restrictive environment:* By law, children with disabilities or with special needs are eligible to take delivery of proper education carefully formulated to cater for their special needs. In an event where the type of disability is such that the child with disabilities cannot thrive in a general education

classroom, even with accompanying supports and cares; only then would the school be required to separate the child with disabilities from their counterparts without disabilities.

- *Create environments and opportunities for evocative participation:* It is required for schools to create a learning environment filled with various opportunities for parents and students to mingle and interact throughout the course of the special education process.
- *Set up bureaucratic safety measures:* Schools are required to provide practical safety measures aimed at ensuring that the rights of children with special needs and their parents are protected. Furthermore, schools are required to institute rich steps geared toward addressing quarrels. Practical safety measures ensure that parents can take part in meetings, scrutinize all educational methods and records, even going on to obtain an individual educational evaluation.

Looking at the IDEA's Part B, it would be observed that it spells out the requirements needed for education for children with a disability ranging from ages three to twenty-one.

(ii) Americans with Disabilities Act: The Americans with Disabilities Act (ADA) of 1990 delivers civil rights safeguards to people with disabilities. In this Act, a person with a disability is described as someone who possesses a physical or mental impairment, which, in turn, significantly restricts him from engaging in one or more critical life actions; a person who possesses a record or history of living with such an impairment, or a person who is observed by other people as having such an impairment. The Americans with Disability Act, however, does not name all of the impairments that are covered in detail.

Quoting from Title II of the ADA, it would be seen that the Act *"prohibits discrimination on the basis of disability by public entities, including public elementary, secondary, and postsecondary schools, regardless of whether they receive federal financial assistance. Title II requires that qualified individuals with disabilities, including students, parents, and other program participants, are not excluded from or denied the benefits of services, programs, or activities of a public entity, or otherwise subjected to discrimination by a public entity, by reason of a disability."*

The Department of Justice provides access to the full text of the ADA and other material about the act on their ADA website; they also provide lists of questions and answers about childcare hubs and the ADA Amendments Act of 2008 particularly formulated for *Students with Disabilities Attending Public Elementary and Secondary Schools.*

(iii) Section 504 of the Rehabilitation Act of 1973: Section 504 of the Rehabilitation Act of 1973 is focused on protecting the rights of people with disabilities when it comes to programs and activities that are financially assisted by the federal government, as well as federal funds. Beneficiaries of these funds may range from public school districts and institutions of higher education to other state and local education agencies.

Section 504 supports children with disabilities to have access to school services by calling for schools to make accommodations and adaptations available. The Act, however, does not make provision for individualized education programs, which other Acts like the IDEA cover. In some cases, a child might not be eligible for special education services under the IDEA, but the same may be allowed special accommodations with this law. For instance, a child who uses a wheelchair for mobility may not require special education services but would be protected by Section 504.

The guidelines executing Section 504 in the educational institutions' framework can be seen at 34 C.F.R. Part 104. This all-inclusive list of over forty frequently asked questions and answers about Section 504 and the education of children with disabilities further elucidate how this law adequately protects your child.

(iv) Antibullying laws: The federal government's antibullying laws describe bullying as unsolicited, hostile behavior exhibited by school-aged children that consist of an actual or supposed power imbalance.

The Department of Justice and the Office for Civil Rights (OCR) have categorically said that bullying may constitute harassment when it is centered on a person's color, race, national origin, sexual orientation, religion, or disability. Some behaviors that are considered as harassment may include:

- Undesirable conduct, such as verbal exploitation, name-calling, appellations, slurs, or spreading rumors.
- Threatening to do harm or cause injury
- Undesirable graphic or written statements
- Physical attack

Other such behavior that may be physically hostile, injurious, or demeaning

Bullying has become the topic of increased media attention in recent times, chiefly as technology has opened a window to "cyberbullying," sometimes with catastrophic penalties.

Even though about 20 percent of students in America reported having been bullied at one time or the other, the numbers show that children with special needs and children with disabilities encounter more bullying than most.

- Pupils with learning disabilities, such as health impairments, autism spectrum disorder, speech or language impairments, and emotional or behavioral disorders, report higher degrees of victimization compared to their peers who have disabilities. Reports also indicate that their victimization stays consistent over time.
- The prevalence of bullying differs for specific types of disabilities; an assessment shows that of all the cases of bullying reported, over 35 percent came from students with behavioral and emotional disorders, almost 40 percent came from students with autism, 24.3 percent came from students with intellectual disabilities, 20.8 percent came from students with health impairments, and 19 percent came from students with peculiar learning disabilities.
- Studies have indicated that pupils with special needs were more concerned about safety in schools, being hurt, or hassled by their peers compared to students who do not have any form of disability.
- When reporting bullying, pupils in special education were urged by their peers not to tattle almost twice as frequently as pupils not in special education.

But thankfully, every state in America, as far back as April 2012, had enacted antibullying legislation, with the exception of Montana. The law comprises eleven key components, specifications on proscribed behavior, formulation, and application of local education agency policies, training, and preventive education.

(v) School policies: It is not strange for individual schools to formulate policies linked to bullying, discrimination, and harassment. It is therefore expedient that the parent gets conversant with such enacted school policies which should typically be contained in the parent handbook, policy manual, or could simply be obtained by visiting the guidance and counseling unit of the school.

The Department of Justice provides a Guide to Disability Rights Laws for the purpose of further educating parents and caregivers on whatever areas they might want to inquire about: whether information on the laws protecting children with disabilities or guidelines for schools, institutions, and work areas.

(b) Parents Doing What It Takes To Protect the Rights of Their Children with Disabilities

With the exception of schools that are run by religious organizations and those that get little or no federal funding, all schools should be covered by one or more of the aforementioned laws discoursed above. This implies that children with special needs who have peculiar needs are lawfully protected in most school settings.

Regrettably, the presence of potential legal protection is one thing, but the implementation of the same is another. However, parents can take deliberate steps to ensure their wards get the lawful, peculiar protections they need in school.

- *Understand your child's disability or special needs:* You need to get a comprehensive understanding of your child's disability and special needs if you are to stand a chance of adequately explaining them to your preferred education provider. Typically, the best way to cultivate a robust understanding of your child's disability or special needs is by frequently speaking with your child's pediatrician. It is imperative to grasp the diagnosis, indications which may include the frequency and duration, treatment, prescriptions, and whether or not there would likely be a need for administering medications during school hours and/or during extracurricular activities.

- *Assist the school in understanding the disability and special needs of your child:* You need to help the school understand the intricacies of your child's disabilities. This would help them properly manage the situation, create the needed peculiar environment, and see how best to engraft your child into taking part in school-sponsored extracurricular activities. The first thing you can do is get in touch with a 504 coordinator, special education coordinator, or other persons nominated by the school authority to take care of cases that are disability and special needs related.

If you demand that a school absorbs and manages your child's disability or special needs, then you have to offer exhaustive facts to the school on the topic of the disability and needs of the child. In some cases, a parent can ask that the school include a health section to their ward's IEP, come up with an Individual Health Plan, or make practical modifications available. These demands can also capture the provision of an aide for your child with special needs.

For the most part, it is central to furnish the school with information that indicates an association between the requested accommodation and the child's special needs. Generally, it might be obvious to a school why a child with, say, the brittle bone disease would need to be given alternative activities to gym time. On the other hand, it would be far less apparent why a child may require more rest breaks than most unless the parent takes time to enlighten the school on the child getting tired quickly. Apart from your comprehensive elucidation, it would be quite helpful if your child's pediatrician would write a confirmatory letter to the school which would help buttress your claims. It must be noted though that the school reserves the right to demand a copy of a child's medical records.

- *Help your child understand their disability and special needs:* One of the fundamental steps a parent should take in helping their child with special needs enjoy their rights is to provide information that is age appropriate. This information would empower the child in advocating for himself whenever the need arises. For instance, a child who suffers from migraines can be schooled to make out triggers or symptoms early on before they begin to drastically affect him. With such information, the child can alert the school and request to see the nurse to take their medicine.

(c) When Your Nurse Worries about Implementation by the School

In an event where a parent or parents of children with special needs disagree with the school authority on the implementation of the school's guidelines or laid down laws by the state on the rights of children with disability or special needs, there are a few things that can be done by aggrieved parents to help them achieve respite.

There is, however, no need for any form of confrontation which could escalate into unpleasant developments. Every society has a number of outlets by which aggrieved parents can seek for the right thing to be done at any given time.

Exploring those options can help with finding justice and peace and might lead to the eventual implementation of the laws as they ought to.

(d) *Organizations That Can Assist a Parent in Dealing with Defaulting Schools*

The pursuit of justice can be made easier and faster when certain organizations are informed and involved. Contacting these organizations that focus on championing the rights of the disabled in society can go a long way in swiftly solving the problem. These organizations can regularly provide advice for ensuring that a school meets the disability and special needs of a child. Some of the well-known organizations that are committed to providing information about school-related disability and special needs include the following:

- United Cerebral Palsy, www.UCP.org
- American Diabetes Association, http://www.diabetes.org/
- Epilepsy Foundation, http://www.epilepsyfoundation.org/
- National Alliance on Mental Illness www.nami.org
- Bazelon Center for Mental Health Law http://www.bazelon.org/

(e) *Getting Further Help:*

When you encounter a school that refuses to accommodate or offer services required to effectively meet your child's disability or special needs, or so much as exhibits the slightest form of discrimination against your child owing to the prevailing disability, then seeking legal assistance would be a viable solution. The aforementioned organizations might assist in directing you or any of such families to the right legal aid operating within their vicinity.

Families who have children in public schools or any private schools that receive federal grants can explore the option of directly contacting the OCR. OCR makes resources available to ensure that schools meet the disability and special needs of their students in hopes of eliminating all forms of disability discrimination. Also, the OCR makes information about lodging grievances against schools that do not do so, available for public consumption.

Furthermore, every state has a protection and advocacy agency fully mandated by the federal government to handle a selection of disability-related cases. The National Disability Rights Network (NDRN) can provide more information about protection and advocacy agencies located within your vicinity or state.

In an event where you find it hard to amicably resolve your differences with the school owing to their lack of cooperation, you would do well to refer to a disability or education attorney.

Notable Points

(i) *Federal and state legislators have enacted laws aimed at safeguarding the rights of your child with special needs, some of which include;*
   o *Individuals with Disabilities Education Act*
   o *Americans with Disabilities Act*
   o *Section 504 of the Rehabilitation Act of 1973*
   o *Antibullying laws*
(ii) *Individual schools have also done their bit by formulating policies that would further protect your child's rights.*
(iii) *If you have concerns over the violation of your child's rights, you can contact various nonprofit organizations who would help you in advocation or assist in litigation.*

(iv) The government also has open doors when it comes to reporting special needs violation in any way. You can contact the OCR or NDRN to lay formal complaints and to seek redress.

Actionable Steps

(i) Get a pen and notebook and write out any other state of federal law you know that helps protect your child with special needs.

(ii) Take some time out to further research on the ADEA, ADA, the Section 504, and any relevant laws discussed.

(iii) Write out ways you can help your ward's school strengthen their special needs laws.

(iv) Write out other organization that might assist you in protecting your child.

– – –

Chapter 4
Broaching the Subject of Mortality with Our Child(ren)

(a) Understanding and Addressing the Fears/Worries of the Child

The subject of death is sometimes hard to talk about. Nevertheless, death is an inevitable life experience that is bound to happen to everyone. You, as a parent taking time out to discuss the subject with your child will help them understand the experience, do away with any forms of misconception that they might have picked up along the way, and know how to handle it when the time comes. A robust communication strategy around the subject will make a whole lot of difference in a child's ability to manage the experience when confronted with the reality of the same.

There would be an urge to hold on until you and your child may have had an experience of death before you decide to discuss the subject, owing to the fact that, for you, the subject may be too sensitive to simply discuss at any time, thanks to the high levels of emotion prevailing at the time. This strategy, in most cases, might be extremely counterproductive. First, waiting for an experience could result in the wrong timing for discussion. While mourning, you and/or your child would not be in the right frame of mind for such a discussion, and your child would have too much to deal with all at once.

Secondly, death isn't something anyone could readily predict. Waiting too long could result in never getting the opportunity to do it. There are cases where the parent passes on before ever getting to educate the child on the subject of death and dealing with such losses. So it is ideal for parents to waste no time in helping their children grasp the subject of death, no matter how awkward they might feel about it. Death should be a topic which you discuss openly with your spouse and kid(s), because when children have no preparation, they often respond with excessive fear, anger, or confusion.

A healthy grasp of the subject of death is equally important for parents if they must be able to properly teach their wards about the same. There is simply no justification for trying to teach a child something that you do not understand. Parents owning up to their dispositions about death will aid them in talking more amenably and in all conscience to their children, giving them room to fine-tune the volume of information to the maturity level of their wards.

(b) Looking at the Myths behind the Descriptions of Death

For most people, the topic of death is an enigma. This is because the subject comes with a lot of dark and grey areas— areas that can be best described as paths whose destinations are mostly unknown. As a result, more than a handful of myths and fallacies have been propagated over the ages.

Believing and holding tenaciously to any of these incorrect theories can promote needless guilt, distress, or anxiety. However, having a healthy view of the subject of death—what to anticipate and what is typically a part of the experience—can aid in mapping out a thorough and peaceful transition from the various levels of grief. Here are five myths about death that have prevailed over the ages and the truth about them:

Myth One: *Not being present when a loved one passes away is tantamount to absolute failure/disappointment.* For many people, not being present at the bedside of a loved one just before the latter makes their final transition is unforgivable. To them, such an action is proof of a lack of love, loyalty, and devotion. Sharing the moment alongside family would help reinforce the existing love and affection toward the dying and the family being left behind.

But the issue with this belief is that death itself remains a complete mystery, as far as timing and occurrence are concerned. For some people, death happens with absolutely no preparation or awareness, while for others, families and loved ones are well informed and prepared for the grieving process. Regardless of how death comes, it would be unfair to be too hard on one's self or others simply because they couldn't make it over in time to witness the transition at the final moment. Life can be tricky; we do not always get what we want.

Myth Two: *Everything has to be done to stop a loved one from dying.* For some people, the passing of a loved one is an experience they wish to keep at bay for as long as they possibly can. For them, if every invented technology and cure is not deployed, or if the dying person on life support is deliberately taken off the machine keeping them alive, then a great disservice has been meted out to the person. This would also imply that those who are responsible for such decisions have essentially "killed" the person.

Death shouldn't necessarily be associated with negativity; it does not always have to do with the passing of the young and promising, or the dying of people who ought not to. Sometimes, age or protracted ailments can be behind the death of a loved one, not the people who are responsible for taking care of the dying. While innovative cures and technologies are being developed and are becoming more accessible, this does not imply that those options would always work and save the ailing person. In some cases, aggressive "cures" only serve to further protract the ailment and dying process rather than save lives.

Myth Three: *All healing is in food and water; so ensure the dying keep eating and drinking.* As strange as this may sound, there is a widely held belief that all health and healing emanates from what we eat. While this belief can seem like a stretch, it can also be dangerous.

People who believe this often think that by making sure that the sick and dying get access to the "right kind of foods," then the inherent healing properties locked in what is being eaten can be accessed to trigger complete restoration to their ailing body, thereby eliminating the possibility of death. This can create an atmosphere of false hope that makes the eventual grieving process a lot harder even when medical practitioners try their best to keep the involved parties informed.

Myth Four: *The ideal place for people to die is within the four walls of infirmaries.* This belief holds that hospitals are the best and most ideal places to pass; the thought of any demise outside an infirmary implies that the deceased died prematurely or could have been saved if only he was taken to a hospital in time.

It is not uncommon for individuals to die in their homes, lying on their beds with people who care for them, tending to their needs and listening to their last wishes. Hospitals can indeed help a great deal in diagnosing what is wrong with patients who are admitted, but hospitals cannot save all their patients from dying. Again, for some, a home might be best described as a private nursing home, a supported living facility, or a rest home residence. Regardless of who is involved, a home scenery is typically more serene for both the elderly and their families. Many families would treasure such a passing that happened at home compared to it happening in the hospital.

(c) Understanding How Children View Death

Depending on the developmental levels of children, their perceptions about the finality of death would differ significantly. This implies that approaching the subject would depend on the level of understanding of individual wards.

Typically, there are four concepts of death:

- *Irreversibility concept:* Here, death is seen as a permanent situation. It is something that cannot be reversed, no matter what's done.
- *Finality concept:* Here, death is viewed simply as the ceasing of the active function of the body; the body stops all functions once it experiences death.
- *Inevitability concept:* This view of death holds that death is something that everyone must experience; this belief goes beyond just people and includes animals and insects as well.
- *Causality concept:* Death is seen as something that happens only when there is a cause; it is hinged on a theory of consequence.

It is important to explain these concepts to children so that they can understand and cope with the loss of a loved one when it does occur.

(i) How babies and toddlers view death: In reality, babies and toddlers do not fully grasp the idea of death. However, they can sense what their parents feel in the event of the demise of a loved one. This is why during a period of grief, it is advised that parents maintain their usual daily routine while taking care of themselves. Psychologically, sticking to a routine serves as protective energy that stabilizes them in times of key emotional disruptions. In times of grief, endeavor to provide added physical care, comfort, a sense of security, and avoid unnecessary separation.

(ii) How youngsters view death: For most youngsters, death is a temporary thing. This way of viewing the experience is not surprising at all as most youngsters get a healthy dose of reinforcement of such delusion from cartoons and programs designed to amuse children of their age range. The prevalence of concrete thinking within the minds of young children causes them to see and hear things just as they appear and sound, respectively. It is therefore essential that clear and direct language is engaged when telling them about death. The use of euphemisms must be completely abandoned. Phrases like, *"he has passed away," "he has gone to the great beyond,"* or *"he has gone to sleep"* should not be used to teach them, as such phrases would not be comprehended and could even create fears associated with sleep or travel.

Alternatively, sentences such as, *"She has died; this means we will not be seeing her again,"* can be used. It is advised that you keep giving them clear messages even when they keep asking of the deceased weeks or months after the loss. This should be done with gentility and calm language while giving room for in-depth explanation depending on the questions that follow. They can be consoled with the fact that the memories of the deceased will forever be with them. Parents may also decide to use religious explanations, and that is acceptable. However, for young children, using religious explanations exclusively tend to leave a few things to be desired as they would continue to seek more concrete, detailed explanations about the physical realities of their loss.

For most young children, their lack of vocalization of grief often shows up when they play; for them, play is a language. This implies that parents must pay attention to what their young kids try to communicate to them via play.

(iii) How school-aged kids view death: This category of children tends to view death as what it is—as a final experience. However, they do not necessarily understand that it is a universal one. For a school-aged child, it is imperative for you to be unassuming and candid when discussing the topic. Also, with them, the parent ought to inquire about what the child understands. Time must be invested in the dislodgment of any form of misconceptions or misunderstandings.

Furthermore, the parent should be open and sensitive to the demands that may come from the young child in terms of the need for support in finding the appropriate words to express emotions while finding plausible solutions to warding off unhappiness. This can be achieved by giving the child constant openings to express their feelings. At this point, listening would be more profitable than talking.

School-aged children also may still be too young to comprehend some aspects of death, such as the causes and implications. In addition, it is normal for them to give a human face to death—calling it by names such as the boogeyman or ghost. On some occasions, school-aged kids might unconsciously relate the passing of a loved one to their own failure; this means they may accept as true that they are partially or totally to blame for the demise, thereby nursing a great amount of guilt in the process for what happened. If this is the case, then the parent needs to be deliberate in putting forward assurances that completely exonerates the child. It is also important to highlight the fact that nothing they do can reverse what has happened or bring the dead back.

In the event where the young child loses a significant adult, there is likely to be an emergence of fears of potential abandonment or neglect within the child's mind. These fears can show up in strange behaviors, such as the child needing more cuddles, more bonding, and even possessiveness toward an adult.

- The child must be reminded that not every sick person would end up dead.
- Take time to assure the child of the parent's health.
- Emphasize how many loved ones the child has that are currently alive and well.
- Encourage the child to engage in activities that would help reduce anxiety.
- Be thoughtful, allowing the child to grieve and to express such grief the best way they see fit.
- The parent should take care, surrounding one's self with adequate support.

Parents should note that young kids have a keen sense of observation; their rapid healing would be dependent on what they see and make of their parents' healing. This implies that the best way to take care of the young child is for the parents to take care of themselves.

(iv) How adolescents view death: The understanding of death by juveniles is not too different from how adults understand it. However, they may resist the urge to show their emotions about it. Since the thinking capacity of teenagers is typically at the early stages of formulating abstract thinking, finding meaning in death and contemplations on bigger questions about life may both be a struggle and a central thought in their minds. This would typically cause them to cast off restrain, and engage in risky activities, feed their guilt within, or bottle up anger over being alive or their lack of control over life and death.

It is important for the parent, while exercising enormous amounts of patience, to uphold the highest expectations of healthy behavior. The expression of anger, guilt, or fear should be done in ways that do not jeopardize the child's well-being.

The child should be encouraged to freely express their feelings, while the parent provides support and guidance where necessary:

- Encourage exercising to help reduce tension.
- Play soothing music or give cold baths to help them calm down.
- Employ the use of journal writing, sketching, and/or other innovative channels to give room for expression of emotions.
- Open up to friends and family. The advice of professional psychologists will also help.
- Formulate healthy individualized coping strategies that the child can adapt by observing you in practice.

What Will Happen to my Special Needs Child When I am Gone

Notable Points

(i) *A lot of myths surround the subject of death. It is important for you, as a parent, to separate the wheat from the chaff so as to be well equipped to teach your child about death.*

(ii) *There are four worldviews on the concept of death, namely:*
- *Irreversibility concept*
- *Finality concept*
- *Inevitability concept*
- *Causality concept*

(iii) *Understand how your child sees death and try to lead them along the path of further understanding.*

(iv) *Your child will communicate their feelings when grieving in various ways. You have to be sensitive and help them walk through the process.*

(v) *Once you child understands the concept of death, it would help them transit as quickly as possible.*

Actionable Steps

(i) *Write down any myth about death that you or members of your household might still be propagating.*

(ii) *Assess your child with special needs and write down how you think they view the concept of death.*

(iii) *Write down ways you intend on going about correcting their wrong impressions about death.*

Write your observations about their use of emotion to communicate grief.

— — —

Chapter 5
Broaching the Subject of Mortality with Your Child(ren) Continued

(a) *Guidelines for Speaking To Children with Special Needs about Death*
  (i) **Prepare the child beforehand:** To prevent the breaking news of the demise of a loved one from coming with so much shock, it is advised that the child with special needs be told long before it happens. This will prepare the child's mind for the event when it does occur.
  (ii) **Employ the use of certain words:** The right words can help smoothen the transition from a regular conversation to one involving the subject of death. Choosing words can help minds that are very concrete and literal in their thinking to properly interpret what is being said. Avoid tricky words that might water down the gravity of the conversation; also avoid words that might make the discussion altogether unbearable.

(iii) Emphasize celebratory memories of the deceased's life: Encourage children with special needs to remember fond memories that trigger feelings of laughter, joy, and gratitude. The child might express their thoughts about the deceased, but do not compel them if this does not happen.

(iv) Be part of the child's transition: Some children have a knack for rituals when it has to do with death, which helps them obtain closure on the subject; this is perfectly normal. Activities ranging from writing stories about the deceased, performing a symbolic salute, to holding a candle out for a moment, and saying a few good words in prayers can help the child make peace with the experience. If the child with special needs is a nonverbal child, then the parents should help him/her collect valuable items that would help connect to the pleasant memories of the deceased, such as pictures or items. The child can then choose to visit those collected items now and then to honor the memory of the deceased.

Another thing that can help speed up the healing process is to identify places where the child with special needs used to go to or activities which the child used to engage in with the deceased. By visiting such a place or engaging in the activity with the child while talking about fond memories of the deceased, the parent would give room for a rapid transition.

(v) Allow regular visitation of the ailing loved one with the child: Allow the child to visit the dying loved one. This will help the child build closure and establish fortitude when death eventually occurs. It is equally important to prepare the mind of the child

before the visit; some situations may be too graphic for the child, and people around the dying person might not have optimism on their faces. If the child declines to visit, such a decision should be respected. In addition, a parent can explore other options that technology provides, like phone calls, video calls, and the like.

(vi) *Be patient with the child and listen:* The child may have a lot of questions, some of which would be weird, repeated again and again, and seem unnecessary. The parent must be committed to attending to the child's inquisitiveness. It is important to point out to the child that some questions cannot be rightly answered at the moment but would be later on in life. This can help in tackling the difficult questions asked. Be patient with the child who may ask the same questions over and over again.

(b) *Common Issues That Arise After the Death of a Parent*

The passing of a parent can be an extremely emotionally challenging situation. Not many people can identify with the feeling of losing their father, mother, or both; nevertheless, everyone at some point has to experience some kind of mortal loss. As much as knowing that the death of one's parents is unavoidable, it does not in any way make the experience less grievous or easier to handle. The impact of losing a parent can forever change a child, no matter the age, and this can happen biologically and psychologically.

Findings in the field of neurology have shown that the loss of a parent would prompt physical distress in the short term, while grief would expose the body to greater levels of risk in the long term. Quite a number of studies have established connections between diseases such as cardiac challenges, immune syndromes, and even cancer to unsolved grief. Even though it is uncertain why grief would cause such dreadful conditions, a prevalent theory suggests that a continually stimulated sympathetic nervous system, which is also referred to as the fight-or-flight response, can bring about long-term heritable alterations. Such crucial changes, if left unimpeded, can promote deregulation, which is one way cancerous cells grow.

Unlike the typical appearances of the physical symptoms that show up after the demise of a parent, which could be described as comparatively consistent, the psychological effects are generally unpredictable. Emotions, which may include but are not limited to fear, sadness, anger, rage, shock, nervousness, guilt, regret, and sorrow are expected to be seen and experienced by the bereaved child in the years following the loss of a parent.

The use of psychological data to adequately grasp this particularly agonizing grief has proven to be impossible, as grief has diverse effects on individuals. But imperial research has indicated that the areas of the brain most impacted after the loss of a parent are the posterior cingulate cortex, frontal cortex, and cerebellum. These areas are linked with memory storage, appetite, and ruminating on past events.

Another thing that contributes to the impact of the death of a parent is the indisputable fact that while growing up, the presence of a paternal and maternal figure plays a key role in the overall development process of children in general and children with special needs in particular. The influence of both parents in the shaping of the emotional and psychological contents of their children is extremely vital. Unfortunately, this idyllic model of a family is not always obtainable for all children in society. Thanks to the many eccentricities that exist in our society today, a sizable number of children are able to lead happy and healthy lives without necessarily having their biological parents as caretakers.

A 2015 study carried out in the United Kingdom showed that an estimated twenty-three thousand six hundred parents pass away each year. This statistic implies that one parent dies every twenty-two minutes. These parents leave behind a sizable number of dependent children; the same study also showed that about forty-one thousand dependent children (aged between zero and seventeen) are left behind by their dead parents. This implies that one hundred and twelve children get bereaved every day.

Again, studies indicate that mortality rates do differ by geography and social standing; this means that children living in poor areas are more likely to lose their parent(s). Furthermore, certain kinds of grief are more likely to affect some categories of children. For instance, the rates of mortality among children with disabilities who have inherent multifaceted health needs are greater than among the overall population. This implies that young people who are admitted to special schools are more likely to experience bereavement of a family member compared to their peers who attend mainstream schools.

A child whose parent or both parents have passed away, who has to experience growth without a comprehensive family structure will meet varying degrees of difficulties. Research has shown that these challenges would especially escalate in the period of adolescence when the child is trying to formulate an identity. This aberration would go on to possibly affect their life over time. It is understandable that not every child who loses a parent will end up with psychological or social challenges; but the sad reality remains true that living without a parent can bring about undesirable effects, which will ultimately impact the child's adulthood.

For that reason, paternal deprivation causes a halt in the child's physical and spiritual needs, resulting in the emergence of many other problems.

Here are a few problems that might come up:

(i) *Behavioral Complications*
1. **Absence of life skills:** Some of the most important lessons in life are learned by children through the sheer observation of their parents over time. Life skills such as the need to love, to remain resolute in the face of hardships in life, to esteem and preserve their environment, to defend self and loved ones, to attain success, to earn respect, money, and the likes. In the event that there is a parental deprivation, so that the figure whose part it is to build the child's academic and social skills become absent, what follows would be a deterioration and deceleration in the learning of these skills.
2. **Taking part in delinquencies:** Due to the impact of their losses, coupled with the many abnormalities which life throws at them, it is commonplace for children who have lost both parents to use rage and anger amongst other strong emotions as coping mechanisms and ways to express their feelings. This can often create a downward spiral if not well handled and can even lead to disastrous behaviors.

Children who are livid, owing to disenchantment and the feeling of being abandoned, might choose to express their feelings in ways that are inhospitable to their surroundings. This anger could lead to antisocialism, putting them in pole positions and getting involved with the wrong peers, like gangs, in which they are typically encouraged to display violent and lawless behaviors. Such terrible choices could inevitably lead to issues bordering around criminality.

3. *Engaging in substance abuse:* Despite the level of sensitization of the negative effects of substance abuse on the body's health, a lot of young people today still wallow in the grip of substance addiction. This fact is even more worrisome among orphan youth.

   The numbers when it comes to the consumption rate of cigarettes, alcohol, and drugs among orphans are particularly high. Studies indicate that 14 percent of cigarette consumption is by individuals from broken families, while alcohol addiction data for individuals from broken families stands at 18 percent.

   A different study also indicated that 50 percent of heroin addicts were found to have come from broken families. These facts imply that the average child who grew without parental presence and supervision is vulnerable and could be endangered if the case is not properly handled.

4. *Sexual snags and complications:* The loss of a very influential parent could lead to a series of problems concerning the sexuality of a young person. A lack of guidance and answers could lead to harmful explorations, thereby risking exposure to early pregnancies, sexually transmitted diseases, confusions about their own sexual identities, and body dysmorphia among others.

5. **Psychological health complications:** Some of the psychological challenges that orphaned children face include the following:
    - Morphological development disorders
    - Difficulty in communication
    - Sensitivity to physical touch and uncomfortable disposition to eye contact
    - Ingestion and slumbering disorders
    - Prevalent phobias, stress, depression, anxiety, anger
    - Recurrent ailments such as headaches and stomach problems
    - Suicidal thoughts and feelings

    Other unpleasant occurrences that may be related to some level of psychological complications may include excessive crying, bedwetting, excessive dependence, thumb sucking, abuse of others, and lots more.

6. **Academic retrogression:** Research findings have indicated that children from single-parent families make poorer grades when paralleled with children who come from complete families. This implies that separation of children from parental figures either due to death or divorce can negatively impact their learning.

    The ability of a child with special needs to concentrate on learning can be very sensitive; little changes can greatly alter this balance. Losses can trigger the wrong emotions that would initiate these changes for the worse. Correcting this downtrend can prove to be very challenging if the right initiatives aren't taken before the very inception of the loss. In many cases, therapeutic solutions are employed, but the need for such extreme measures could be greatly reduced if certain things are done earlier before the child experiences such a loss.

(ii) Emotional Complications:

The death of a child's parent(s) can alter the course of their emotions in ways that would negatively impact them throughout their life. It is important to understand that once the emotions of children are vigorously shaken by such events as the death of a loved one, many things kick in.

(a) *Vulnerability on issues of trust:* Children see parents as protectors and providers. This means the sudden disappearance of one in any family can bring in a twist of role description in the minds of the children. Such loss can breed misery and distrust. Such a flow of emotions can leave children vulnerable, unable to protect themselves when confronted by the challenges of life. Also, handling certain questions could prove to be tough and could further breed fear; questions like, "Who is going to be responsible for earning money for the house?" "How should the family go about maintaining the livelihood in the house?" "Who should be looked up to for protection for their siblings?" The abundance of fear might trigger the rapid development of various kinds of anxiety disorders in these children.

The absence of trust or a capacity to build the same in a child while growing up will create difficulties for the child later on in life as they attempt to navigate relationships and build meaningful connections. A child that doesn't understand the need to trust others will constantly live in fear and anxiety. He will hardly form amicable alliances and friendships with people around them, and doing business would be impossible.

(b) *Privation of affection:* Growing up surrounded by people who shower affection can be one of the best things to ever happen to a child. The very definition of love and support is taught to a child by sheer example. When such affections are freely shared amongst members of the family, the child can associate usage with practice. From infancy, babies, children, and adults who get love from loved ones, especially from parents, come to rely heavily on this peculiar bond. However, the loss of one or both parents at such a critical point when they are in dire need of affection can significantly alter the life of the bereaved child for the long haul. This vacuum would not only leave these kids in a vulnerable position but can lead to disastrous consequences. The employment of alternative parental figures such as close relatives, or even foster parents is mostly adopted; that too can prove to be an uphill task in itself as there would be a lot of struggles between the child and the new caregivers to reestablish boundaries of giving and receiving affection.

The problems associated with the privation of affection can range from the affected children derailing from taught family values to clinging to the wrong people in an attempt to quench the thirst for such love and affection.

(c) *Developing an inferiority complex and low self-esteem:* Another challenge that might come up as a result of a child losing a parent or both is for the child to begin to think of himself/herself as being too weak and not worthy of attention compared to their peers. This is a sad reality; the child observing their peers getting love and attention from a parent while theirs is absent can deal blows to their child's self-esteem. Soon, the child would begin to harbor such thoughts that reinforce the idea that they are deserving of love, attention, parental commitment, and guidance. Eventually, a well-rooted inferiority complex forms, which then goes on to play key roles in the child's thinking and decision-making ability.

(iii) Social Challenges

The development of children includes how they perceive and live amongst people and the society. The death of a highly influential person like a parent can greatly impact how the child relates to social rules and norms. This can make the child antisocial and unwelcoming to others and anything that might be beneficial to their well-being.

1. *Troubles in adhering to social rules and norms:* In a model scene, the role of parents as caregivers, role models, and front-runners is very important. They are responsible for helping chart the best course for their wards by employing discipline and consistency every day. In any case, parents provide the first stage of learning for their children: from rules to values and methods of living. Where faults, blunders, and weaknesses occur, it is attributed to the parents being the key agents of correction and empowerment.

However, studies have indicated that children, particularly those raised by single parents, are most likely to face problems associated with sticking to social norms, rules, and guidelines. This has been observed more with boys who no longer have father figures around them. The issue of rebellion, noncompliance, and maladaptive behavior, especially when an attempt to create a new authority figure or system emerges, could become rampant. So, the surviving parent begins to struggle to keep the child in line, resulting in more fights and outright distancing from such authority by the child.

These acts of rebellion are often subtle cravings for attention by the child, howbeit in the wrong manner. It is not unusual to see such happen. When identified, they shouldn't be ignored but rather resolved to help understand and straighten out the underlying issues that cause such behavior.

Notable Points

(i) *It is important to prepare your child beforehand, discussing the subject with deliberately chosen words, while laying emphasis on fond memories of the deceased.*

(ii) *Be an active participant in your child's transition, letting them choose to visit the sick loved one prior to death while being very patient with the child.*

(iii) *Behavioral and social complications can occur when a child loses their parents and doesn't fully transit through the grief.*

(iv) *It is important that grieving be carried out systematically to help protect the child.*

Actionable Steps

(i) *Write down any approach to explaining death to your child that you deem as workable.*

(ii) *Write down any methods that you feel might help your child through a smooth transition.*

(iii) *What other challenges do you imagine could befall a grieving child?*

(iv) *Write down your thoughts on emotional overdrive for a child in grief.*

Chapter 6
Managing Grief

When you lose a loved one, grief is almost inescapable. Most times, the process is completely unpredictable as loss can trigger memories and emotions that may have been compartmentalized and sidelined with time. It is perfectly normal to grieve. However, if you feel like no progress is being made, then it might be best to seek the help of a professional to help you through the process.

Grief can be described as a response to any kind of loss; it usually incorporates a variety of emotions, from profound sadness to anger. Typically, the process of acclimatizing to a substantial loss might radically differ from person to person, contingent on conviction, background, connection to the object of loss, and added factors. Grief isn't limited to the death of individuals alone; it can include the demise of a pet, the termination of a union, and separation with a family affiliate, or any other form of loss.

The purpose of grief counseling is to assist the bereaved to grieve in a way that can be seen to be normal. It is intended to help the person grasp and deal with the emotions being

experienced, eventually finding a way to move on. This can be achieved through
- Existential therapy,
- Individual therapy,
- Group therapy, and/or
- Family therapy.

(a) *Stages of Grief*
- Repudiation
- Irritation
- Negotiation
- Dejection
- Recognition

Notable researchers on the subject of these stages of grief acknowledge that the bereaved can go from one stage to the other, with some even experiencing two or less before finally acclimatizing.

While there have been a number of other models of the stages of grief, the symptomatic reactions and manifestations are generally the same. Here are a few in no particular order:
- Shock and skepticism, feeling numb, denial of the loss
- Sorrow, anguish, isolation, feeling empty
- Guiltiness, remorse, embarrassment
- Annoyance, offense
- Timidity, fear, weight loss

Experiencing these symptoms is normal, but intense manifestations for a prolonged period of time might indicate an abnormality, hence, the drafting of grief counseling or grief therapy.

(b) The Values of Grief Counseling

For most people, there is usually no need for a grief counselor to help them walk through their grieving process. However, others who find the transition a bit challenging would benefit immensely from the skillset of a grief therapist. In the event that the bereaved have suffered psychological challenges before the loss, or if the level of grief enters a chronic stage, which then begins to inhibit normal activity, then grief counseling can assist in addressing the flow of strong emotions, thereby triggering the healing process. In addition, just like it is with most practices of therapy, the procedure proves to be most functional if the affected individual seeks help voluntarily and is willing to put in the work and make progress.

(c) Managing Grief

- *Do not self-isolate:* It is important to stay connected with others during periods of grief. Support structures may comprise of household members, acquaintances, religious leaders, a grief support group, and/or a licensed grief therapist to assist in the process. Support structures can assist in the following ways:
    - Help with putting together funeral arrangements or with household tasks.
    - Perform various faith-based mourning rituals that could help in finding peace and comfort.
    - Mingle amongst people who can relate to grief.
    - Create a safe atmosphere to transition from grief to acclimatization.
- *Practice self-care:* While reeling from a loss, it is normal to ignore hygiene and self-care. Overlooking one's self impedes the process of transition in many ways.

Remember to
- Get involved in doing something creative that would help in the expression of feelings: activities such as writing, painting, forming a scrapbook, or playing an instrument.
- Get adequate rest and exercise; this will help with the elimination of physical and emotional fatigue.
- Give yourself room to heal. Be patient and let yourself go through the motions.
- Understand what prompts the grief, and be prepared for their occurrence.

Knowing that grieving can be peculiar to individuals and temperaments, the aforementioned tips can help tremendously in the management of grief.

- *Adult grief counseling:* The primary goal of any grief counseling session is to assist the client to incorporate the realism of their bereavement into their lives going forward, while also helping them to keep a strong bond with the loved one that passed away. Clinically, two vital steps must first be taken:
  - recounting the event-story of how the death occurred. This must be done within a calm and safe space. This is meant to help the bereaved face certain aspects of the story and let go of areas of hurt.
  - Opening the back story of the relationship between the bereaved and the deceased. This will direct the client to learn how to rebuild the bond with the deceased rather than surrendering it.

(d) *Grief Counseling Techniques*
  - **Allow talking:** Let the bereaved talk about the departed person—ask questions that would prompt

the person to speak about the deceased in a safe space.
- **Be sensitive:** The bereaved might be experiencing deeper levels of grief/trauma. The counselor needs to distinguish between the two states.
- **Deal with guilt:** Guilt can stop a person from moving on. It is important to deal with such guilt and help the bereaved repair their sense of worth and value. The bereaved must be encouraged to forgive themselves.

(e) *Grief Counseling for Kids and Young People Living with Disability*

Grief counseling for children and those with disabilities can be challenging. Nevertheless, it is an exercise that should be done with great emphasis on love and clarity. Exceptional care must be given to the details of such an exercise, as it involves children and assisting them in grieving in a healthy manner.

Here are a few tips to help lead a child through the grieving process:

- It is important to respond to any questions that they may ask about death—even the seemingly tough ones. Candid and loving responses are preferred, using words that are suitable for their age grade.
- Allow the child to choose how best they prefer to say goodbye to the deceased. Embolden them to work through their grief in ways that they see fit.
- It is important to talk about and recollect memories about the deceased. No need to make them avoid such thoughts or memories, as this can help them become open about their feelings.

- Be respectful of various grieving styles. Children grieve differently, even if they are from the same home and are going through the same loss at the same time.
- It is important to allow the kids to have their train of thought about grief. Avoid telling them how they ought or ought not to think, feel, or act while grieving.
- Encourage them to speak during the memorial service of the deceased. It would help them let out some degree of emotion and help them see how loved the departed was to others. If they decline to do so, respect that. Instead, help them take part in their preferred goodbye ritual.
- Children with special needs may choose to show their grief and feelings differently from other children. This disparity in expression does not trivialize the depth at which they are affected. Here are a few strategies that can come in handy when dealing with your grieving child with special needs:
    - Form a habit of looking at pictures of the deceased together. This serves as a valuable pastime, where you can reflect together and share memories.
    - Make a habit of sending greeting cards to the child. This will reassure the child that you still care.
    - Embolden the grieving child to wear an outfit that may be a link to the deceased.
    - Craft out a pillow or blanket from the deceased person's clothes, and allow the child to develop a liking to it.

- Share the deceased person's favorite music.
- Create a book about the deceased.
- Dedicate a day to light a candle in memory of the deceased.
- Create a memory box. Allow the child to determine what memories would be placed into the box.
- Spend time reading books like Badgers Parting Gifts together.
- Get the child ready for the funeral. Tell them what to expect and how to behave.
- Spend quality time together. This will help with the transition.

Here are a few guidelines for dealing with grief issues peculiar to young people with autism:

- Note that reactions to bereavement by individuals with autism can be extremely peculiar. This implies that the method of support must be unique as well for it to be effective.
- People with autism may share the same reactions to death and grief. This may include repudiation, anger, and despair.
- The process of anguish for people with autism may be strongly impacted by their disabilities.
- The employment of skilled care is a vital factor in assisting persons with autism to move their grief to acclimatization.

It is problematic to make a sweeping statement on how each child will react to loss through death; however, such losses of loved ones can give rise to obsessions, fears, phobias, a decline in understanding, and struggle with change. This can be regarded by others as being unfitting reactions or even coldhearted indifference. Kids on this scale rest on the security that comes from familiarity. Often, these kids may have to struggle to put words together that would clearly express their feelings. This is why goodbye rituals can be extremely helpful.

The parent must balance how much information is given to the child, as too much or too little information may lead to further confusion for the child and may make it hard for the child to voice out apprehensions or even ask the right questions. Once information overload is allowed to flourish, the child might then end up developing medical anxiety and depression.

It is important to be sensitive and know when exactly to employ the skillful help of a professional. Sometimes, the grieving process might stall, which is normal, but an outright halt is what must be avoided as it could be counterproductive. Get in touch with a professional

- when the child insistently denies that anyone has passed away or continues to behave as though nothing happened.
- when the child threatens or talks about suicide. This is particularly problematic as many people with autism also have a history of depression and may have suicidal thoughts.
- when the child becomes abnormally and importunately violent or begins to take part in antisocial activities.
- when the child becomes unusually withdrawn and chooses social isolation.

Notable Points

(i) Grief is a very sensitive issue to deal with and must be handled with a lot of courage and foresight.

(ii) Some manifestations of grief can be physical and obvious, while others are not. The non-conspicuous should not be mistaken for lack of the same.

(iii) Managing grief can be done through self-care, a deliberate resistance to self-isolation, and participation in adult grief counseling.

(iv) Various techniques like talking, being sensitive, and dealing with guilt can be deployed in an adult grief counseling session to help with your transition.

(v) Sometimes, professional help can help a child with special needs to transit, which is if the parent does all that is required and sees no progressive result.

Actionable Steps

(i) Write down your thoughts on grief.

(ii) Write down what other ways you can employ in the effective management of grief.

(iii) What methods have you found to be most effective in managing your child in times of grief?

Write down when you think would be the best time to seek professional help in managing grief.

Chapter 7
The Uphill Task of Single Parenting

More often than not, the life of a single parent becomes a bit more challenging upon the passing of a spouse, especially when having to care for children with special needs. The challenge of going on to cater to the kids alone can be very overwhelming for the single parent. In no time, bills begin to mount, the pressure to perform both roles press in, and the fear of the unknown creeps in.

There are a number of challenges that single parents commonly face as a result of the abrupt passing of their spouse. These challenges, if not resolved on time, could ultimately ruin relationships with their children, immediate and extended families, friends, and loved ones. It is important to review some of these challenges as this will help identify them and think of how to go about resolving them for a better future.

(a) Single-Parent Families Owing to Death or Separation

A strong family unit helps in the impartation of a sense of membership in everyone involved with that family.

However, the family can begin to experience a deformation when there is a divorce or death of a parent. As a result, many questions arise from the minds of the members of that family as to whom they belong with, particularly when it involves the case of separation. Where the custodial or non-custodial parent is alive and well, but due to a divorce, is no longer considered a member of the home, the children may be confused about who precisely their family members are and where their overall standing lies.

Looking at the sudden passing away of a parent, one must admit that even though there are a number of events that hold significance in the life of a family, the death of a parent is perhaps one of the most significant points and can bring about a series of situations and issues. When the parent is an elderly adult, the passing is, to some extent, predictable and can be considered as a normal part of life. But when a young child loses a parent that is at the prime of life, it can be unthinkable/unexpected and an occurrence that changes the child's life forever.

Regardless of whether the single status of the parent came about due to death or by divorce, raising the children single-handedly remains an overwhelming task, going by the setting of a disobliging community. There is an excess of childcare and domestic chores to handle, while time and energy remain limited for the parent to go about developing themselves and meeting their own basic psychological necessities.

Apart from the day-to-day economic struggles, single parents battle the rising social expectations, which partly anticipate the total collapse of the family and that the children will be worse off. But statistics for the devastating presence of poverty in single-parent homes indicate that, following the elimination of social expectations, the differences in modification between single-parent homes and model homes disappear.

(b) The Financial Struggles of Single-Parent Families

A 2011 study revealed that children being raised by single parents are largely more in the offing to live in poverty compared to children being raised in typical couple families. Over 47 (47.6) percent of children in single-parent homes were poor in 2011 as equated with over 10 (10.9) percent of children living in traditional double-parent homes. Furthermore, over half of all poor children in 2011 were being raised by single-parent households.

(c) Poverty and Resources

The 1997 and 1999 data analyses indicate that the poverty rate was around 30.9–43.1 percent, greater amongst single-parent households than amongst two-parent families, with single motherhood being the sturdiest determining factor of female poverty in the United States. Again, estimation points out that virtually half of the single mothers who live in poverty—30 percent of women who gave birth to their first child out of wedlock live in poverty as compared to 8 percent of women who had their first child within the setting of matrimony.

A large number of single mothers in America rely heavily on government aid in the form of welfare. Studies have shown that about 75 percent of single mothers who are teenagers receive welfare within the first five years of giving birth. Forty percent of adult single mothers live below the poverty line, and nearly 60 percent depend on welfare payments or food stamps after giving birth. Single mothers, in general, stay poor much longer than divorced mothers. Although divorced mothers are given welfare for a maximum of three to four years, the single mother is far less likely to ever stop receiving welfare, thereby making her unlikely to ever exit poverty as receiving welfare has proven to decrease women's employment, which is a key element in a possible path out of poverty.

Findings from an experiment conducted indicate that single mothers reacted to income assurances by considerably decreasing their work effort. Welfare benefits are also linked with a reduction in marriage rates, lessening another trail of exit from poverty. A $100 upsurge in monthly welfare benefits for single mothers lessened her probability to get married by 2.5 to 5 percent. According to another study, 80 percent of single parents continued unmarried for another two to four years after first getting payments from welfare packages.

Another research indicates that approximately two out of five households headed by a single parent live in poverty; this rate is substantially higher than that of married-couple families. Furthermore, research shows that single mothers are more likely to quit a job for family, health, or other provisional reasons.

This kind of data contributes greatly to a growing myth that children being raised by a single parent may be less likely to possess the pecuniary and emotional stamina required to grow and thrive. For a selected number of researchers, however, single parenting is a way of life that has the capability of producing strong families, mostly if complemented by sufficient and wide-ranging systems of support, regardless of it being bumped in by structural and fiscal hardship.

Regardless of outcomes, single parenthood is gradually becoming more widespread. Studies indicate that since the

1980s, the ratio of deliveries to unmarried women has increased to 27.8, 51.3, and 71.6 percent for Caucasian, Latina, and African-American women, respectively. As much as these rates continue to soar, so are concerns about single parenthood as well, especially as it has to do with their financial security and that of their families.

(d) Gender Factors Associated with Single Fathers

It might be thought wise to deliberately include single fathers in the conversation while attempting to discuss the subject of single parenting in general. After all, single parents, without any regard to gender, all face particular challenges that are unheard of for married couples. Recent data from the United States reveal that one in four single-father homes face food insecurity; this rate is almost double compared to conjugal-couple homes. Nevertheless, single mothers do have higher rates still; this goes on to signify that gender-based dynamics also play a significant role.

As well as being more common, statistics show that single mothers find themselves more probable to being paid less income and even owning fewer assets compared to single fathers. Even though the gap between gender wages has tightened in recent years, other issues like work-related discrimination, average weekly pays, and period out of the workforce continue to underwrite the gender-wage gap.

(e) Wealth, Assets, and Financial Flexibility

Statistically, single mothers possess a median wealth of about $100. This is a far cry from what their male counterparts get and amounts to only 4 percent of the median wealth of single fathers ($25,300). Single mothers who had never gotten married were statistically worse off economically by the time their children got into the first grade compared to other mothers. Research further articulates the significant role that prosperity and affluence play in families; it serves as a cushion to privation and a liftoff pad to any economic successes in the future.

In addition, as at the period that their children are born, the economic standing of single mothers who were over age twenty bore a resemblance to that of teenaged single mothers more closely than it bore a resemblance to that of married mothers their age. These values were evaluated by poverty status, income-to-needs ratio, welfare use, workforce input, and conduct.

A closer look at research numbers would reveal that there is a need for grave concern for the life projections of single mothers and their families. The probability of moving upward on the income ladder (economic mobility) is very challenging for the wards of single mothers. Quite a collection of researches also reveals that children of single mothers are more probable to get involved in dangerous behaviors, like drug abuse and unguarded sexual activities. However, one of the enduring contests of understanding this data is the strain in separating to what degree these results are socioeconomically contrasted with directly attributing them to the marital status of single mothers.

A lot of single mothers struggle to achieve economic stability due to a variety of complex reasons. The discussion about how to go about addressing these challenges must capture income inequality and the analysis of wealth.

Children being raised by single parents have far less family pay and are more probable to wallow in poverty compared to children in a two-parent household. In actual fact, children of single teenage mothers expend more time being poor compared to children in any other family setting.

Still, children in single-mother families are more likely to receive most forms of public aid.

Children in single-parent households have reduced economic mobility, making them less likely to ever make an income which tops that of their parents compared to children of two-parent and divorced-parent households. Fifty-eight percent of children of mothers who have never gotten married, whose income is rooted in the bottom third of the income distribution make an income in the bottom third of the income distribution themselves. Ten percent of these children get to move to the top third of the income dissemination chart.

It is postulated that if the marriage rate of 1971 had been maintained at the same rate, then the poverty rates would not have gone up. Rather, it would have had an overall reduction of 4 percent adding in marriage-related changes. Thirty-seven percent more black children and 67 percent of white children being raised by single mothers would have been lifted out of poverty had the parents decided to get married.

So going by prevailing data, it must be admitted that the death of a loved one does deal blows to any family, no matter how closely knit. This even hits children harder as they are often too young to understand the intricacies of death and life without the deceased. But particularly, children with special needs must be given special attention, as the shock from such a tragic loss can further plunge them into deeper physiological and psychological problems. It is important, as a parent, to help them see death the way they ought to, prepare them for the inevitable, and allow them grief and transit to acclimatization in the best and shortest way possible.

With these statistics, it is important to do the needful as parents in preparation for any sudden passing of one or both parents. It is also vital to set up modalities for the smooth running of the life of your child with special needs when you pass. This is to ensure that they are well taken care of in your absence.

Notable Points

(i) It has been statistically proven that raising a child with special needs as a single parent is extremely challenging.

(ii) Most single parents find themselves in this precarious position due to a lack of adequate knowledge and planning.

(iii) Children being raised by single parents are likely to live in poverty compared to their counterpart typical couple families.

(iv) Over 47.6 percent of children in single-parent homes were poor in 2011 compared to 10.9 percent of children living in traditional double-parent homes.

(v) Poverty rate is 30.9–43.1 percent greater amongst single-parent households compared to two-parent families.

(vi) Single motherhood is reported to be the sturdiest determining factor to female poverty in the United States.

(vii) Forty percent of single mothers live below the poverty line.

(viii) Sixty percent depend on welfare payments or food stamps.

(ix) One in four single father homes face food insecurity.

(x) Children with special needs must be given special attention, as the shock from tragic losses can plunge them into deep physiological and psychological problems.

– – –

Chapter 8
While You Are Here

(a) Taking Note of the Obvious

One of the most important steps that parents need to take in order to secure the future of their children with special needs is to do all that is within their power while they are still alive and able. Since death can be unexpected and has no respect for our wishes and desires, it is important to do more for the child in a variety of areas, knowing very well that one would not be around forever.

Several things could be done in preparation for when the parents or caregivers of children with special needs pass away, so that the children aren't plunged into difficulty as regards surviving, getting access to all that is due to them as inheritance, trust, or societal and/or governmental aid. Like every other venture, this task must begin from the foundations starting from when the parent is alive and well and open to making critical changes that can better the child's future.

Typically, there are desired outcomes that every parent has toward their children. These desires are nothing below what every child is expected to experience before entering adulthood. Child outcomes are interrelated within and across various spheres of development. They come from and are boosted by timely compassionate interactions between parents or caregivers and their wards. These timely interactions can birth an enduring reaction to growth across the sequence of life, whereby the role of one sphere of growth impacts another sphere over time.

But for parents to effectively help their children reach these desired outcomes, core childcare knowledge, approaches, and practices must first be put in place. These are strongly linked with effective parent-child relations and the healthy growth of these children.

Here are four desired outcomes that have been identified as being the foremost pursuits of parents for their wards:

(i) *Physical health and security:* One of the basic needs of children is to be cared for in such a fashion that encourages a robust thriving of all their abilities and see to their continued existence and protection from harm, even from bodily hurt. Despite the fact that such security desires are imperative for all children, they are particularly critical for young children, who characteristically lack the distinct resources required to elude vulnerabilities. Instead, young children depend a great deal on parents and caregivers, within and outside the household, to carry out an action on their behalf to safeguard their health and development. At the most rudimentary level, children have to be given care, as echoed in physiological and emotional shields, needed to meet typical standards for physical development, some of which may include things like a guiding principle for optimum weight and delivery of recommended vaccinations. Physical health and security are necessary for realizing all of the other outcomes.

(ii) **Emotional and interactive competency:** Children require care that encourages progressive emotional well-being—the kind that supports their overall mental fitness. This might comprise having an affirmative sense of self, the capacity to manage demanding situations, control emotional provocation, overcome terrors, and accept dissatisfactions and frustrations. Parents and caregivers are critical assets for children when it comes to the management of their emotional excitement, handling, and dealing with various behaviors. They attend to this role by giving positive affirmations, passing on affection and respect, and promoting a sense of safety.

The steady outpouring of support by parents helps to curb the risk associated wit the internalization of behaviors, just like those linked with nervousness and depression, which can weaken children's ability to adjust and function as expected at home, school, and within the community. Symptoms like excessive apprehension, dependence, ineptness, apathy, melancholy, and withdrawal are pointers of emotional troubles that are commonly witnessed among very young children who grow up without adequate parental care.

(iii) **Social competency:** The ability of children to effectively form and nurture connections with peers and other adults depends on how healthy their basic social competency is. Social competence may take account of children's capacity to be in harmony with and respect others, showing complete tolerance to other people's religions, race, ethnicity, sexual preferences, or economic background. It is also entwined with other regions of children's development, such as physical, intellectual, emotional, and semantic.

Rudimentary social skills comprise an array of prosocial behaviors, for instance, compassion and concern for the way others may feel, teamwork, sharing, and formation of perceptions. These skills are strongly linked with children's accomplishments in academic and nonacademic sceneries and can be promoted by parents and other caregivers. They are also linked to children's future successes throughout an array of frameworks in adulthood.

(iv) **Intellectual competency:** Intellectual competency incorporates the skills and abilities required at each age and phase of development to thrive in academics and out in the world in general. Children's cognitive proficiency is distinct by traits such as semantic and communication skills, reading, lettering, calculation, and problem-solving skills. Children profit immensely from inspiring, thought-provoking, and reassuring environments in which to cultivate these skills; this goes on to serve as a foundation for healthy self-guiding practices and methods of tenacity necessary for achieving meaningful academic strides.

All of the aforementioned desired outcomes for children, particularly children with special needs, must be engineered to develop effortlessly before the inevitable exit of any parent or caregiver from the child's life. This would be a worthwhile investment that would guarantee that the future of the child is something they themselves can be proud of. This can be done by providing the right environment, the right education, the right support, and the right health care.

(b) *The Right Environment*

Meaningful growth and development always require the right environment. Humans thrive poorly in unfriendly and distasteful surroundings, let alone youngsters or children with special needs. Parents can make tremendous strides in the progress of their wards if they can be deliberate in making sure that their wards are always surrounded by people and things that trigger rapid growth.

Naturally, setting up the ideal environment would involve the entire family putting their heads together and coming up with various ideas and solutions in a bid to customize the home to serve the child with special needs. These environmental adjustments do not stop at the home alone. It also has to be done by the school and academic environment. Collaboration between the parent and the school authority by way of sharing ideas and proffering solutions can make the process smoother and more beneficial to the child in the long run.

It should be noted that assembling adaptations to accommodate children with special needs must be done with the uniqueness of the child and the prevalent need in mind. Not every child is the same, and each disability will necessitate different adaptations. Childcare providers, in conjunction with parents, should collect as much information as possible about the child and the disability. Also, they must learn about conventional adaptations that can be made. Parents and professionals who cater to the child with special needs can be an incredible resource.

More often than not, simple and easy-to-do adaptations are usually done in order to save time and resources. Also, the modifications stand to profit the other children in the schools' childcare program.

(i) *Wide-ranging modifications to accommodate children with special needs.*

- *Corporate planning:* Before embarking on any modifications within the home, parents should sit with other members of the family and map out a plan together. It would be necessary for everyone to research the topic any way they can before coming together to organize ideas. When setting goals, it is critical to keep them simple, achievable, inexpensive and should match the capabilities of the child.

  For the academic environment, you may lend your ideas and suggestions to the school authority, or even ask to be a part of the crew that cultivates and tracks the child's IEP. With a seat at the table, parents can be part of various discussions and exercises required to reach goals. Discussions reached at this level should then be forwarded to the remaining members of the family by the parents for their input and observations.

- *Play toys and equipment modifications:* Innovative ways can be adopted to modify play toys for children with special needs. The focus should be safety and the simplicity of usage. Keep sharp objects away, eliminate toys that could be swallowed which may cause harm, and make changes that can help the child utilize those toys a little better. Modify toys that the child hitherto finds it difficult to firmly grab, remove whistles from toys if they irritate the child, and so on.

- *Childcare area modified to the smallest detail:* Trivial alterations in the childcare surroundings may make periods a child with special needs passes with the parent or caregiver stress-free and more pleasurable for everyone involved. For instance, a serene, set-apart zone, exclusively prepared for play would immensely assist an overactive child. A child who has challenges with poor vision may profit from the additional lights and strategically placed lamps in the play zone. A child that has motility issues would be very pleased to walk on floors devoid of any kind of slippery rug or covering.

- *Model for behaviors that need assimilation:* Children are particularly good at picking up visual effects. This is why it is encouraged as a learning tool. Some children with special needs however, can be reserved, timid, or indifferent, especially when left to interact with others. The best way to help them is to be an enviable example; the parent or caregiver is encouraged to be a play partner themselves. Craft out plays about pretend shopping, playing board games, or participating in crafts. Your active participation would encourage the child to become more comfortable and much more accommodating; once this threshold is reached, other children could be invited to join in the play activity.

- *Deliberate use of words to identify a playmate and how to be a playmate:* As a way of teaching them to use words to refer to their other peers, it is important to be deliberate when using them around the child. When referring to another child, try as much as you can to look directly at the person being referred to. The direct approach would ground the use of such words in reference to the person and make it easier for them to communicate.

- *Educate other typically developing children on how to talk to and play with children with special needs:* Parents should be conscious of the fact that other children who desire to interact and play with children with special needs may not know how to go about it. Still, for others, their experience with other children with special needs in the past could have left them very skeptical about relating with another. Parents and caregivers need to educate these children on how to get the attention of the child with special needs, initiate conversations, and go about playing and having fun. For instance, gently touching the child with special needs on the shoulder before talking, looking at them directly while doing so would benefit a child with a hearing impairment.

- *Refocus on the strengths and needs of the child:* It is possible to be completely focused on the weaknesses and disabilities of the child with special needs to the point of not seeing potential, progressive growth and what the child might need at the moment to help him improve even more. As much as it depends on the parents and caregivers, you must elude the temptation to become overly focused on the child's disabilities. Interact with the child as you would any other child, as a whole person. Arrange for activities that will back a child's strong points. It is essential for the child to feel positive and capable.

- *Consult with relevant early childhood specialists and health care experts:* Consulting childcare professionals can reduce the risk of imitating any action(s) that could jeopardize the hard-earned progress that has been achieved with the child with special needs. Together, parents, caregivers, and childcare professionals can chart a suitable part in setting up these spaces in a manner that would trigger rapid development in the child over a short period. Do not hold back any questions or lingering fears. Caregivers and professionals almost always know exactly what to do for the ailing child.

(ii) Guidelines for handling food allergies:

Some children with special needs might face the challenge of properly ingesting certain foods, such as cow's milk, wheat foods, peanuts, nuts, lactose, and eggs. Also, some young children might have difficulty breaking down foods with high fiber content. This could be as a result of allergies or peculiar inabilities to handle the constituent compounds from any of these food groups.

The consequences of ingesting foods that cause allergies can vary from child to child, and can go from mild to acute reactions at a given time. These reactions range from minor sensitivity of the skin to very acute symptoms, which might include difficulty breathing. It is important for parents to have a handy list of all their children's allergies and their corresponding triggers; this is because these allergies can be perilous or even life-threatening.

- *Discuss allergies with family and caregivers:* Educate all family members who are likely to come in contact with the child with special needs about all their allergies. This way, they would know to avoid serving the child certain foods that might trigger the allergies. Schools and other caregivers too must be informed before the child is enrolled or accommodated. Discuss things like when the allergy was first detected, the likely symptoms of an allergic reaction, and the level of sensitivity.

- *Always be prepared for an outbreak of allergic reactions:* It is important that the parent knows and educates every member of the household and school about how to manage these allergic reactions, should they occur at any time. Everyone around the child must be prepared with treatment and solutions at hand. Have written instructions handy in case an ambulance needs to be called or if a much milder reaction is to be treated with prescribed over-the-counter medications.
- *Be meticulous about labels, paying attention to content combination:* It is important to always watch what it is that the child with special needs is served to eat. Some children have little or no tolerance for certain ingredients, even if it is served in the smallest quantity.
- *Be mindful of cross-contamination:* Indirect exposure has been known to cause allergic reactions in some children with acute sensitivity. For instance, a child who has a peanut allergy would still experience allergic symptoms if a knife used to spread jelly on their loaf was previously used to spread peanut butter on another child's loaf. Ensure that all tools and food preparation surfaces are carefully cleaned. Do not reuse utensils that have previously touched a reactionary/trigger food. Wash hands thoroughly with soap and warm water if they are used to prepare food that contains an allergen before making contact with the child with an allergy.
- *Consider banning certain foods:* Sometimes, it is best to completely ban the purchase and use of certain foods

within the house. This way, accidents would be greatly reduced. Look for healthy substitutes that the child tolerates, and that would make up for the nutrient vacuum. In some schools, childcare programs do not allow peanuts or tree nuts; this is because allergic reactions to those foods can be deadly.

Notable Points

(i) The four desired outcomes for your child with special needs identified are physical health and security, emotional and interactive competency, social competency, and intellectual competency.

(ii) Setting up the right environment for your child's development is imperative.

(iii) Put up far-reaching modifications to accommodate your child's needs through corporate planning and equipment modifications adjusted to the smallest detail.

(iv) It is important to model exemplary behaviors that can be adopted by your child.

(v) Teach the deliberate use of words to identify others.

(vi) Help other developing children engage your child more effectively.

(vii) Keep your focus on the child's strengths.

(viii) Seek help from early childhood specialists and health care experts.

(ix) Keeping your child with special needs away from food and things that cause allergies is important.

(x) Discuss allergies with contact persons; always be prepared.

(xi) Be meticulous, and give attention to contents. Be watchful for cross-contamination and explore placing bans on certain foods.

What Will Happen to my Special Needs Child When I am Gone

Actionable Steps

(i) *Write down ideas of how you can better the environment of your child with special needs.*

(ii) *Write down how you can go about formulating healthy societal relationships for your child with special needs.*

(iii) *Write down ideas that can help improve social acceptance amongst family, friends, and peers.*

(iv) *Write out foods and things that your child is allergic to.*

(v) *Write down ideas on how best to help them avoid such foods/things.*

― ― ―

Chapter 9
The Right Education

A parent placing their children with special needs in a pivotal position of having a sound education is one of the topmost investments that could ever be given to the child after the parents are long gone. There are a lot of academic opportunities that can help the child academically that you can explore. This way, when you are no longer around, your child would still go on to have a fruitful educational life. Supporting the child to make the transition from one level of education to the other would require cautious planning and widespread research to ensure the school will be right for them.

Early planning is crucial for the parent while soliciting the assistance of various dedicated support groups and government programs.

(a) *Cultivating an Amicable Partnership with the School's Authority*

The foundation for a productive school experience for the child with special needs is in the nurturing of a progressive collaboration between the parents and their wards' school. Taking time out to learn more about the school, its amenities, practices, and caregivers, alongside making vital information about the child readily available will aid in the development and maintenance of ongoing relationships even after the parent is long gone.

Typically, ensuring that communication between parents and the school remains vibrant would require the parent to keep an up-to-date progress report about their child with special needs. Whether the parents and school choose to keep the communication line formal (that is through systematic support group meetings and parent-teacher sessions) or informal (that is through email, phone calls, and quick drop-ins with teachers) makes no difference, provided that the depth of communication continues to be progressive.

(b) Formulating Student Support Groups

Student support groups (SSGs) are formulated to offer supplementary learning to specific students. Typically, this group would come together and come up with workable modalities that would ensure that the student in question receives support that is tailored to meet their particular learning challenges. The composition of the members of this student support group may include the following:

- The parent/primary caregiver (it is recommended that both parents, if present, be part of the SSG)
- The ward's class or homeroom teacher
- The school selected nominee (it is recommended that the principal be part of the SSG)
- A child with special needs advocate (this is optional and should only be considered on the parent's demand)
- The child with special needs (this is optional and should only be considered on the parent's demand)

Adding in the child's learning and behavioral therapist into the SSG can also be a good idea as their professional input may help the group get some key decisions right without having to experiment along with the unknown.

The typical roles of SSGs are diverse, but here are a few to note:

- To ascertain the needs of the child
- To contemplate the need for any form of corresponding curricular adjustments
- To frequently appraise already identified needs of the child on a termly or yearly basis
- To allow the school authority to know about all supplementary educational needs of the child
- To recommend plausible solutions to the school authority that would help tackle the child's prevalent needs
- To come up with an individual learning plan, deliberate over it with teachers and assist in its eventual implementation.

(c) Individual Learning Plans

One of the first jobs of the SSG is to come up with an Individual Learning Plan (ILP) for your child. An ILP is a jointly inscribed document that outlines the present level of ability of a student, identifying unambiguous goals for future accomplishment. With a well-structured ILP, students with learning troubles and disabilities can have their learning carefully tailored in such a fashion to suit their individual needs.

The plan should give attention to the academic needs of your child, but it should go beyond that and also look at their care, social, medical, and personal needs. Furthermore, the ILP should be malleable enough to give room for alterations.

ILPs are only crafted specifically for those areas of the curriculum where the child with special needs would require added educational support. However, it can be made to cover the entire curriculum if necessary for the rapid development of the child.

Usually, an ILP is structured to capture the student's existing level of learning, taking into cognizance the social, philological, and socioeconomic background of the student. ILPs are typically drafted by the student's teacher during an ILP meeting with parents, caregivers, school counselors/nominees, caseworkers, therapists, and anyone else involved in the life of the student.

A typical ILP should accommodate the following points:

- It should comprise of evocative educational programs charting details, able to gauge goals, and the best approaches to go about achieving them.
- It should detail out what can currently be done by the student.
- It should be suitable for the age and development of the student.
- It should have the primary emphasis on the strengths and potential of the student.
- It should designate duties and accountability.
- It should be appraised habitually.
- It should be tailored and founded on the needs and aspirations of the student.
- It should spell out how measurements of progress can be achieved.

(d) Guides to Formulating an Individual Learning Plan

- *Formulate with the needs of the student in mind:* It is important for the SSG to recognize the strong points, skills, favorite learning styles, and interests of the student. Find out the student's drive. This can be done by simply asking the parents and teachers to reflect on the child's learning both at home and in class. Another way of getting to know what motivates the child is to employ the use of student self-evaluation, inventories, and questionnaires.

- *Set meaningful and measurable goals:* When formulating and setting goals, it is important to set them in the long term such that they would reveal learning curves in the regions of academic, societal, and life abilities. Short-term goals, on the other hand, should be drafted to directly connect to the long-term ones. Each goal must be tailored to be relevant to the child.
- *Plan all the way:* It is important to draft in organizational stratagems, which should address the "whens," the "hows," the "wheres," and the "whos." It is critical to state what teaching methods would be employed, what learning experiences would be desired and planned, and what resources ought to be made available.
- *Stay on implementation:* Implementation is imperative. It should be decided who would be in charge of delivering desired results from what part of the plan. An appropriate timeline should also be made and attached to each goal. In addition, an attempt should be made to explore the integration of the ILP into the child's daily teaching practice.
- *Establish monitoring and appraisal:* Through monitoring, strategies that work and those that don't can be easily identified. The ILP should outline how

effectively to go about monitoring the implementation of each strategy. Besides, time should be set aside for appraisal meetings to make amendments to the plan where necessary based on findings.

(e) Programs That Are Crafted for Students with Disabilities

Captured under the Program for Students with Disabilities, public schools that admit students with mild to severe disabilities qualify for funding to support those students. Going through the SSG, parents of children with special needs can apply for this education support funding and would have no problem being considered.

Typically, public schools use funds from the Program for Students with Disabilities to do the following:

- to hire staff who are specialists
- to initiate and sustain professional development
- to provide continued educational support to their staff, and
- to acquire specialist equipment.

Qualified schools can also reach out to the Department of Education and Training via applications for building modifications and installations that would accommodate students with disabilities, like the installation of low handrails, ramps, and other such facilities. The duty of planning and coming up with recommendations for the school authority's approval rests solely on the shoulder of the SSG.

(f) Making a Choice When It Comes to Picking a School

The number of things to consider while attempting to pick the right school for a child with special needs or disabilities can be overwhelming for any parent. Schools must be assessed in terms of their overall vision, historical strong suit and interests, facilities, and the needs which parents intend to see handled. Inasmuch as every child and family is unique, the choice of what school to apply to should meet the parents' desire to meet their child's needs.

Here are a few points to think about while considering available options:

- Will the school accommodate the strengths and interests of the child? Schools can be more academically minded, more focused on the arts, or given to sports.
- What are the wishes of the child? Children with special needs do have their opinions, and it must be sought. They might prefer one particular school to another in terms of comfort. If the choice of the child conflicts with that of the parents, then they must gently explain why they feel a change would be the best option.
- What are your instincts suggesting? It is possible that what a parent feels deep inside about a school could be exactly right. It is important to explore some of the deep concerns and get satisfactory answers before moving on to make a choice. Here are a few actions that, when taken, can help in making the right decision.
- Parents should normalize attending school open days, being part of information sessions, and joining school tours. This would help in getting a feel of the atmosphere of the schools, their facilities, areas of focus, and preferred learning approaches.
- Parents can make arrangements to meet with the principal. Interactions with the leader or member of the highest decision-making body can help get a good picture of the school. The principal's replies to questions

asked and the overall attitude of members of staff should be able to clear any indecision from the mind.

- Check if the physical environment of the schools is user-friendly for the disabled. The inability of some schools to capture the movability and adaptability of children living with disabilities/special needs should help narrow the list of school options for parents. No need to consider a school that has done little or nothing in terms of facilities and building modifications to fit the students with disabilities. However, in the event that the parent feels comfortable choosing a school that hasn't adequately captured the comfort of the disabled in terms of infrastructure adjustment, the parent can speak with the principal first about what modifications could be made to accommodate the child's needs.
- Parents are encouraged to go through the programs and curriculum of the top schools that they are considering. It is important to do this so that the parent can see clear-cut demarcations that the schools have placed between students with disabilities and others if any, and how the school has intended on improving the educational, social, and behavioral needs of their child with special needs.
- Parents should be forward with questions about how the school plans on helping meet the medical or personal needs of their child.
- Parents should inquire about the school's efforts toward the formation of social interaction and its stance on bullying.
- Parents should also consider the distance between where they reside and where the school is located. It is important to inquire from the school if they provide transport support services. Even though the Department

of Education and Training provides some transport support for qualified students with special needs going to specialist schools, there also is the conveyance allowance accessible to students living in rural and regional areas.

(g) Choosing Government Specialist Schools

Choosing a government specialist school isn't at all out of place; they abound all over the country and are, by definition, easier to get to than conventional schools in terms of the well-structured surroundings and tailored curriculum. On the other hand, this may imply that the number and kinds of subjects being offered may be much more limited compared to what is obtainable in conventional schools. Specialist schools have a wide range of therapists on their staffers' list and are deliberate with their building modifications. Class sizes at specialist schools are smaller than those of conventional schools.

Just like it is with other schools, the criteria for gaining admission into government specialist schools must be met before a child with special needs can be accommodated. Parents who desire to enroll their children can contact the principal of their preferred school, or the Department of Education and Training for additional information. Eligibility for travel support to the school, which is generally by a school bus, is dependent on whether or not the child lives within the designated area pegged by the school authority.

(h) Catholic and Self-Governing Schools

Parents who seek to explore catholic or independent schools would have to make inquiries from individual schools. Ensure you ask about their benchmarks for enrollment. While independent and catholic schools are fully qualified for disability funding, theirs isn't quite like that of the funding available in government schools.

(i) Choosing Other Schools

There are a number of ways for parents to go about educating their children with special needs without having to do it the way every other person does it. Some of these ways include:

- Explore dual enrollment. Here, parents can enroll their children with special needs in both conventional and specialist schooling.
- Explore satellite units. Here, parents can seek interventions from special needs educators, tailored learning zones, and amenities within a conventional school, which students with special needs or disabilities can access.
- Explore community schooling. Here, parents can try government-run schools that offer great alternatives to conventional schooling.
- Explore distance education. Here, parents can choose schools that offer admission to students who meet the benchmarks of distance, medical, school referral, or traveler.
- Explore homeschooling. Here, the parents can choose to educate their wards at home, by themselves. This option works as well, but the parents would have to register their children with the Registration and Qualifications Authority or its equivalent within the state of residence.

(j) Support for Disability at School

A wide range of programs and resources are being delivered by government schools to assist students with disabilities. Some supports that could be easily accessed include the following:

- All government secondary schools employ student welfare coordinators to assist students to manage matters ranging from absenteeism, bullying, substance abuse, family conflict, and dejection.
- The Nursing Program instituted mainly in secondary schools sponsors healthy living programs in approximately two-thirds of most underprivileged schools across the country.
- The Department of Education and Training employs student support service officers to care for all students. These employees, who are deployed based on the demand and referral of the principals, range from speech specialists, psychologists, visiting teachers who particularly handle visual, hearing, or physically impaired students, and social workers.
- Students with language disorders are taken care of through the engagement of language support program providers. These employees ensure that students with such disorders are catered for and helped to outgrow their deficiencies in the shortest period possible.
- Staffers who manage students in need of steady, multifaceted medical support also benefit from the school's medical intervention support funding. It provides complementary support for the toll they pay from their salaries.
- For the hearing impaired, The Electronic Communication Devices Scheme offers a subvention to purchase electronic communication devices and training via the Aids and Equipment Program. Other explicit grants are also available for students with vision impairment.

- With the School Care Program, school staffers, in collaboration with the Royal Children's Hospital receive focused training to care for students with multifaceted medical needs.
- The conveyance allowance is available for students with severe multiple disabilities to assist with the costs of travel to school and back.
- If major building modifications are required to ensure your child can access school grounds, the school can apply for special needs modifications, such as ramping through the Accessible Buildings Program.

(k) Managing Concerns over a Chosen School

In the event that a parent becomes concerned about any particular issue at their child's school, it would be best to tackle it immediately without any delay. Generally, schools are very receptive to parents' feedback and would do whatever is necessary to help the situation get under control.

Concerns raised would be tackled in a manner that would uphold mutual respect between the school and parents of students. This implies that the boundaries and privacies of individuals and families would be respected, no matter what.

- Complaints bordering around the program of the child with special needs should be directed to the SSG meeting.
- Complaints bordering around teacher or staff conduct should be channeled to the principal.
- General complaints on dissatisfactions on services offered by the school should be directed to the community liaison officer at the regional Department of Education and Training office.

Notable Points

(i) The best place to start is by having a cordial relationship with your child's education provider, joining an SSG and formulating a befitting ILP.

(ii) A typical SSG should be founded with the needs of the student in mind, should set meaningful and measurable goals, should plan all the way, stay on implementation, and enforce monitoring and appraisal.

(iii) There are a number of programs tailored to effectively educate children with special needs or disabilities.

(iv) Choosing the right school for your child is important, whether government, private, catholic, or others.

(v) You can work with various school departments to help guide you in your choices.

Actionable Steps

(i) Write down creative ideas to help foster a cordial relationship with your ward's school.

(ii) Write down what you think should be advocated in the SSG and what the main focus should be when formulating your child's ILP.

(iii) Write down government tailored programs that are available within your district.

(iv) Write down what you might focus on more when choosing a school for your ward.

– – –

Chapter 10
The Right Health Care

Providing health care coverage remains one of the most vital things any parent would have to go about doing for their children. Typically, when it comes to health care insurance(s), parents ought to be active, as no aspect of the process is as simple as it may sound. Beginning from locating the best possible medical care, to the act of diligently maintaining an up-to-date record of the medical expenses of the children, and ensuring that all medical claims promptly reach the health insurance providers, so that all claims are attended to.

While nurturing a child with special needs or one with a disability, research has shown that having health coverage is generally the best way of coping with expensive medical costs. A better number of the over six million subscribing Medicaid/*Children's Health Insurance Program* (CHIP) children with special health care needs are from low or middle-income households. This is thanks to the program having eligibility rules that capture financial eligibility limits. Statistics also indicate that about 45 percent of subscribing Medicaid/CHIP children with special health care needs do live in families with income below the federal poverty level (that is, families of three earning less than $21,330 per annum), and 79 percent of subscribing Medicaid/CHIP children with special health care needs come from households with incomes below the 200 percent mark (that is families of three earning less than $42,660 per annum).

By enrolling the child into a robust health care plan, the parent would rest assured that in the event where they are no longer alive, their wards would still get the kind of medical attention required. Parents may be largely unaware of the various choices available for their children with special needs as far as insurance coverage is concerned. The options available can range from continuing dependent coverage to public and private insurance coverage. For children with special needs, parents must understand that their wards may be eligible for not just one but a lot of other types of coverage plans. It is imperative for parents, together with their young adults with disabilities to properly look at all options available and pick a robust plan that coincides with their needs.

(a) Health Care Aids for Children with Disabilities

Generally speaking, there are two leading types of health coverage:
- Private insurance and
- Government programs.

Parents should understand that health insurance differs from federal programs like Medicaid and CHIP, even though most people often refer to both as simply insurance. A lot has changed in health insurance in the last few decades. It is recommended for parents to put in due diligence in knowing what there is to know about the subject before choosing any plan and making any commitment.

(b) The Affordable Care Act

The Affordable Care Act (ACA) was enacted in March 2010. It is an all-inclusive health care reform law also referred to as the Patient Protection and Affordable Care Act or Obamacare.

The three primary goals of the ACA are as follows:

- It seeks to make inexpensive health insurance accessible to the majority of people. The law offers subsidies, known as premium tax credits, to consumers. This lowers costs for families with incomes between 100–400 percent of the federal pegged poverty level.
- It seeks to grow the Medicaid program to ensure all adults with income are lower than 138 percent of the federal poverty level. So far, over fourteen states have gone ahead and expanded their Medicaid programs.
- It seeks to support groundbreaking medical care carriage methods intended to generally push down the costs of health care.

(c) The Effect of the Affordable Care Act on a Child's Insurance Coverage

- Insurance plans can now be bought from the Health Insurance Marketplace if one's employer doesn't offer any health insurance plans.
- During an open enrollment period, one can sign up for insurance on the Health Insurance Marketplace. This signup window stays open for a few months every year. In the event of a loss of one's insurance due to unforeseen circumstances, family members can still sign up at another time of the year. It is important to note that other insurers have their

enrollment periods too. To sign up, parents would have to check with their employers or the insurance company directly.
- It would be illegal for any health insurance company to refuse to cover, owing to one's preexisting condition. This implies that they are legally bound to cover children with disabilities or having special health care needs, along with any forms of mental health disorders.
- Insurance companies are obligated by law to have insurance plans covering mental health care.
- Insurance companies are obligated by law to have insurance plans covering prescription medications.
- Insurance plans can typically cover a child until they turn twenty-six years old. This can even go on longer depending on special health care needs.

(d) When the Child Turns Twenty-Six

It is common for children to grow out of their parent's health insurance plans, and this isn't something to worry about, because they can still be covered. In the event where the physical disability or mental health of the child inhibits them from ever being independent, the parents might be able to maintain the child on their policy. This can be done by furnishing the insurance company with proof of the child's disability.

(e) Dependent Coverage

Thanks to the ACA, parents can now maintain health insurance coverage for their dependent relatives until age twenty-six. Some states even offer more generous dependent coverage, like they have in the state of New Jersey, where dependent coverage is up until thirty-one years of age. Alternatively, parents can explore the *disabled dependent provision,* which insures the dependent for an indefinite period on the condition that the parent remains employed. With this plan, though, parents need to act fast before the child turns eighteen, as that would make them ineligible.

(f) Rudiments of Child Disability Insurance

For many parents, navigating the health care system can be a difficult task, and the use of strange nomenclatures and diverse terms can be tiring. Below is a list of things to note that will help you get clarification, understand how some of the things are done in health care, and hopefully find the right path to getting the best coverage.

- *Referral:* This is a term used when the parent's doctor gives written consent for the child to see a specialist. A referral is typically written and must be forwarded by the doctor to the insurer before payments can be made for the visit.
- *Deductible:* This refers to imbursements made by the client before the insurance benefits begin paying. It is common for there to be set amounts to be paid for some medical services in order to meet one's deductible.
- *Coinsurance:* This refers to a fixed percentage of the medical fees that the client has to still pay once the deductible is met.
- *Copayment:* This refers to imbursements made by a parent for the child who is covered by the same insurance. It is usual for people to pay set amounts for services such as prescriptions or doctor's appointments.
- *Premium:* This refers to the fee(s) that the client, their boss, or both pay for their insurance every year.

- *Point of Service (POS):* This is a bloc having some of the structures of health maintenance organizations (HMOs) and preferred provider organizations (PPOs). Children must have a primary doctor, and seeing out-of-network providers is allowed.
- *Managed Care Plan:* This is a brand of insurance that works with particular health care professionals like doctors, therapists, and specialists; this plan makes health care inexpensive for their clients. Some instances of managed care plans include HMOs, PPOs, POS plans, and exclusive provider organizations (EPOs).
- *Preferred Provider Organizations (PPOs):* With this arrangement, the child with special needs would be allowed to see providers referred to as in-network and out-of-network providers. However, the true cost benefits are seen only when providers within the network are maintained. But with this, there is no need for any form of referral to see specialists.
- *Health Maintenance Organizations (HMOs):* Typically, the parents can only have their wards see certain doctors covered by their insurance. This arrangement, however, ensures that by getting a referral from the child's primary doctor, the child could be taken to see other specialists.
- *Exclusive Provider Organizations (EPOs):* Here, the child is allowed to see providers that are exclusively within the parent's insurance company's network. However, a primary care doctor or a written referral to see other specialists isn't needed at all.

(f) Insurance Programs and Government Health Benefits

Insurance programs and government health benefits can assist households to get health coverage or insurance at very inexpensive and almost free rates that typically cannot be gotten from other health insurance providers. Below are a number of different program types available:

- *Medicaid:* This is a program driven by the government, which arranges for medical services for the general public who are eligible by reason of certain income or disability requirements. There are different packages of Medicaid programs.
- *Medicare:* This is a government-driven insurance program targeting individuals who are sixty-five years and older. It also covers individuals eighteen years and older who have disabilities or special health care needs. The latter category, however, must be eligible by meeting certain requirements.
- *Children's Health Insurance Program (CHIP):* This is a program that affords low-cost coverage for children who are eighteen years old or younger. The charges are dependent on family income levels.
- *Social Security Disability Insurance (SSDI):* This is assistance for young children whereby monthly stipends are given to them based on personal or parental earnings. The young individual or their parents, however, must have paid sufficient social security taxes.
- *Health Insurance Premium Payment:* This is a program that assists families in the payment of their health insurance with the conditions that a member of the household would either get Medicaid or private health insurance through their jobs.

- *Waivers:* Waivers are Medicaid funds used by states to provide long-term services to people with special health care needs, disabilities, and the elderly to assist them to live comfortably in the community. Being dissimilar from other programs, waivers are not a class of insurance; instead, they are founded on the needs of the beneficiaries, not their income levels. Waivers, however, take quite a while to be delivered. So it is often recommended for people to sign up for other programs while they wait.
- *Supplemental Security Income (SSI):* This is a government program that is financial need-based. It aids the payment of living and health care expenditures for children with special health care needs and disabilities. It is possible to be approved to get Medicaid and still go on to also be approved to get SSI.
- *Children with Special Health Care Needs:* This is a state-driven program that affords additional health care assistance for children who have disabilities and are below the age of twenty-one, children with special health care needs, and individuals with no age restrictions, who are ill with cystic fibrosis.

(g) Harmonizing Benefits in Case of More Than One Plan

It is common for a child to be eligible for a private employer plan as well as Medicaid or Medicare. With multiple coverage plans for a child who has quite a number of disabilities, the child is adequately surrounded by aids that can benefit them for a long while. But if more than one plan is in place, the benefits must be harmonized to ensure smooth billing by doctors, hospitals, and pharmacies. In the event where a doctor doesn't accept Medicare, an opt-out letter can be forwarded alongside the bill to the private insurance company. Furthermore, if a doctor doesn't accept Medicaid, and the child is primarily covered by a private plan, the doctor's office can work with the insurance company on how to bill out-of-network as secondary. Parents can equally ask the billing department to bill both insurance plans. This will make the most of the settlements to the provider, as well as decreasing costs for parents.

(h) Top Advice for Any Health Care Benefits

- Parents should have a thorough understanding of their family's insurance or benefits policy. Such knowledge would serve as a road map to managing payments for services. Issuance policies are documents that elucidate what is covered and what is not. These documents are typically given at the point of signing up or can be downloaded from the insurance company's website. Studying this before an emergency occurs can make a huge difference.
- You can get around the complications of health insurance and coverage by hiring the services of case managers. It is recommended to check with the insurance plan or health care benefits program for case management and support. Case managers assist with advocacy and navigation of the entire process. In the event where a case manager is not available, parents can still call and ask their insurance company any questions about their plan.
- It is important to explore all choices before registering. Take a critical look at what the plan covers: doctors, psychotherapy, medicines, services, and so on. In the event that a parent has more than one option, it is recommended that a thorough

comparison be made before a final settlement for the one that best covers.
- If the insurance or Medicare refuses to approve a service that is needed by the child, the parent is encouraged to appeal such a decision. It must be clearly understood that such service is within the boundaries of one's right, and such denials can be overturned.

Notable Points

(i) Two leading types of health coverage are common today: they are private insurance and Government programs.
(ii) The ACA was enacted in March 2010. It is an all-inclusive health care reform law.
(iii) Parents should read extensively about health benefits offered by law for their children, as such knowledge will help them maximize each plan and find relief.
(iv) Some health plans go well with others and do complement each other. But the onus is on the parent to understand and act.

Actionable Steps

(i) Write down a list of private and government health care programs that your child is currently enlisted in.
(ii) Write down your thoughts about the effectiveness of each plan.
(iii) Write down how you were able to successfully harmonize all plans your child is involved in.
(iv) Write down modifications you intend to carry out in order to further help your child's health.

Chapter 11
The Right Support

Some parents prefer to keep the special needs or disabilities of their child a secret. This can give an impression of shame or guilt, regardless of whether or not the best objectives were intended. Sharing such a burden with family and friends can help others understand the challenge and contribute their quota in helping the child with special needs lead a normal life. Lacking knowledge, family, and friends might not fathom the disability but may keep thinking that the child is simply lazy or hyperactive. As soon as they are alert to the true situation of things, they can offer their support for the child's progress.

Amongst family members, some might have reservations about the kind of treatment that their brother or sister with a learning disability is getting from their parents, even if they admit to understanding that the learning disability fashions special challenges. Parents can check these feelings, taking time out to reassure their children of their love and affection.

(a) *Support of Siblings, Friends, or Relatives*

It is important for parents never to underestimate the kind of help that can come from friends and family, both nuclear and extended in helping their child with special needs have a good life. Occasionally, siblings who have come of age, friends, or relatives could be keen and capable of becoming caregivers of the child. These kinds of decisions are not only major but expensive as very few people with special needs or disabilities ever become completely independent, with many having medical or mental health needs that have the potential to gulp down quite an amount of money in terms of treatment costs.

So if a parent ever gets an offer from a family member, a friend, or distant relative agreeing to take care of their child with special needs when the parent is absent, then it is imperative to plan out the logistics beforehand and unambiguously communicate such to the volunteer, eliminating any possible assumptions. Below are a few things to think through:

    (i) *Money:* An important question to consider is where would the funds used to cater to the children with special needs come from? Parents can put some money aside in savings, take out life insurance, or else make certain that a substantial amount of liquid cash is available for the needs of their child with special needs. It is also vital to properly secure the money in a special needs trust account to avoid embezzlement and misappropriation. If such an arrangement is fitting for both the parent and the volunteer sibling, friend, or relationship, then the parents must make sure the caregiver becomes the legal trustee of the trust once they are gone.

    (ii) *Location:* Will the child with special needs be moved to the volunteer caregiver? Are there any needs, considering that where the child presently stays has

been fully tailored to assist them in living comfortably? Moving the child with special needs would incur additional costs of moving, remodeling the new location to be tailored for the child's needs, and so on. It is recommended that the choice of location should rest on the parents' shoulders, who are expected to make the best decision after looking at any and all factors and scenarios available to them.

(iii) *Services:* Typically, adult services are subsidized by the state of residence of a child with special needs, and such funding differs extensively from state to state. Parents should consider what level of funding and services are available in different locations before making any decision to that effect.

(iv) *Stability:* One of the biggest challenges of most people living with special needs or disabilities is that they can be very sensitive to change. For such people, the less the change, the better for them. This implies that when they are separated from their loved ones, maybe by reason of death, and a drastic change is imminent, they go into a "battle" state in order to adapt to the best of their abilities. So this ought to be considered and discussed by the parents and the potential caregiver. If the individual with special needs is a grown-up, holding a job, or is actively involved in activities within the community, then sudden changes such as leaving town would be counterproductive. This needs to be worked out or discussed before it happens.

(v) *Desires of the adult on the spectrum:* While some adults with certain special health care needs, such as autism, might find it problematic to plan through

likelihoods for the future, many would be able to do so judiciously and thoughtfully. Either way, parents must include their adult child with special needs in any planning for their long-term benefit.

Additionally, it's also central for parents to manage records containing a list of all service providers, funding, evaluations, and medical needs of their child. This is so that if a sibling or a caregiver is required to take over in a hurry, all relevant information should be available for them to use.

(b) Maximizing Community Support

One thing parents must do for their young adult with special needs is to help them become actual members of the local community. Sadly, some members of the community who nurture adult kids with special needs choose to live in relative isolation, struggling to uphold a probable and monotonous life for the benefit of their child with disabilities. This can lead to further withdrawals from the child, making them antisocial, not taking part in activities involving family or friends.

Parents can help children with special needs develop robust connections with people that can last a lifetime:

- Take out time regularly and pay social calls to the community library. Ensure that the librarian calls your child by their name. Also, explain to the child how to locate and check out the books and videos they fancy.
- Register at the YMCA. This is an exceptional resource for children and adults with disabilities. They are typically willing to make minor accommodations in programs that could otherwise be challenging.
- Help the child grow in their area of strength. It is important to nurture the skill of the child with special

needs; if the child is good at playing an instrument or singing songs, if they are into sports, love woodwork, or if they love to cook or read, the parents must help enhance those skills and abilities. It will take work at first, but over time, the child will be appreciated for their skills.
- Think through being a part of a religious community. Churches, synagogues, mosques, and other religious organizations are set up to be highly inclusive. Many families count on their religious societies in trying times.
- Consider the option of residing in a town or city rather than a suburb. It is important to note that for most adults with special needs, they find it challenging to fit in well into a suburban community. On the other hand, a single adult with special needs might find friends or at least a community in a city or town, where it is possible to get around without necessarily having a car, see the same people on a consistent basis, and link up with others around similar interests and hobbies.
- Become mindful of support and programs in and around the area. Most cities offer a variety of services and support to people with disabilities. Possibilities range from low-cost carriages to meal services to volunteers willing to help with annexation of arts programs, sports, or other activities.

Notable Points

(i) Once a relative offers to assume guardianship of your ward, such a decision must be considered with prevailing factors like funding the move and stay, the proposed new place of residence for the child, the availability of services, the overall stability of the child, and the desire of the child with regards to the move.

(ii) Engaging yourself and the child in community activities can open you all up to embracement by the community.

(iii) Visit public places, register with community groups, explore religious bodies, encourage your child to participate in their areas of strength, stay within a locality that is closely neat, and take advantage of community programs tailored at aiding children with disabilities.

Actionable Steps

(i) Have a discussion with your child, and write down their thoughts on mingling with people, strangers or no.

(ii) Write down what you can do to help strengthen your child's bond with your community.

(iii) Write down creative efforts you would put in place as touching
- public places
- community organizations
- religious bodies
- sports and leisure
- others

(iv) Write down what you consider to be your biggest hurdles in having effective rapport with your community.

Chapter 12
Development Assessment and Journaling

Assessments every so often consist of numerous tests, both standardized and criterion-referenced. But testing, however, is not the only way used to gauge aptitude. Assessments are appraisals and might be made up of anything ranging from simple observations jotted down to complex, multi-level procedures like a group of teachers amassing a huge portfolio of one's work. Then there are assessments that are needed by distinct schools, districts, or states that assist educators to define whether or not a student is qualified for special education and, if so, what types and rate of services will best back a student's success.

Below are some of the most common assessments in special education:

(a) Individual Intelligence Tests

Here, individual intelligence tests are given to a student one-on-one.

    (i) Wechsler Intelligence Scale for Children (WISC): The school psychologist typically oversees this test,

which gauges a student's acumen in a multiplicity of areas, as well as semantic and spatial intelligence. This is a norm-based test, where the student's performance is gauged against the performance of students at many grade levels.

(ii) *Stanford Binet Intelligence Scale (derived from the Binet-Simon Test):* The school's special education team oversees this test, which is also norm-referenced. The questions are intended to assist educators to tell apart between students performing below grade level due to intellectual disabilities and those who do so for other reasons.

(b) Group Intelligence Tests

Group intelligence and attainment tests are frequently run in the common education classroom. It is via these types of tests that a teacher might first suspect a learning disability. These tests have dual functions: to measure academic aptitude and reasoning level.

(c) Skill Evaluations

Specialists like speech pathologists and the child's general physician use definite diagnostic measures to determine a child's unpolished motor skills, fine controlling skills and hearing, sight, speech, and semantic abilities. Teachers characteristically refer parents to a pediatrician or specialist for a complete physical evaluation as part of the practice of collecting the evidence necessary to cultivate an IEP.

(d) Developmental and Social History

This narrative assessment is formulated by the child's teacher, parents, doctor, and school specialists. Checklists might be filled out, questions answered, interviews conducted, or reports written, aimed at addressing the assets, challenges, and development of a child over time. The focus will be on issues like health history, growth milestones, hereditary factors, bonds, family relationships, pastimes, and the behavioral and academic performance of the child.

(e) Observational Records

Anyone working directly with the child can make information about the child's academic performance and behavioral concerns available. These records can be daily, weekly, and monthly observational records that show a child's performance over time. Typically, the general education teacher has a firm idea of how a child's work and behavior compares to that of other students of the same age and grade level.

(f) Samples of Student Work

A binder comprising assignments, quizzes, schoolwork, and projects can make available a snapshot of a child's aptitudes and challenges in performing grade-level work. A more detailed portfolio for an in-depth investigation could be requested. Here, the contents would include research projects, written assignments with several drafts, or samples of work throughout a thematic unit.

(g) Who and What Is Involved?

The first person to carry out an informal assessment is characteristically the classroom teacher. All the same, a guardian or pediatrician might begin the assessment process. A classroom teacher or pediatrician might demand a referral to a medical specialist, therapist, or psychologist to focus on a certain area of unease. Written records of findings should be kept, along with detailed descriptions of any deliberations relating to the child. Informal and formal evaluations should be done by the special education department or student study team. Formal requests will be made to the classroom teacher and other individuals working with the child to submit any evidence gathered.

(h) Why So Many Assessments

Educators need numerous measures to make sure that they gain a clear picture of a student's performance as associated with others at the same grade level. This process is vital since a student might do poorly on a particular assessment owing to performance anxiety or a learning disability, but a different measure might show that the student can function at grade level given certain settings. For instance, some students do below par on standardized tests but do well in reliable assessments.

(i) What Does It All Mean?

There is no one-off evaluation that can gauge a child's full range of assets and weaknesses. Assessments give educators directions on how to deliver the best services for children, but they are not the whole thing. Parents or teachers ought to provide multiple assessments on an ongoing basis. They can create short-term and long-term goals for the child.

For instance, if it is observed that the child struggles to meet grade-level benchmarks in writing, then focus should be broadened in the contexts in which the child writes, offering numerous opportunities for engaging in authentic practice.

(j) Journaling/Documenting

Journaling is maintaining a journal of thoughts, plans, ideas, thoughts, sketches, or pictorial representations of what is burning within one's mind. As a parent who nurtures a child with special needs, journaling can be fun if done the right way and with the right attitude and purpose.

Journaling has proven to be very therapeutic. It serves as an outlet for thoughts and ideas that keep bickering in the mind. It is also a fun activity, as putting one together would take some time but would turn out beautifully, even if the user isn't as artistic as they would like. Furthermore, journaling can help to organize/streamline thoughts, goals/plans and can help reshape one's outlook to life and assist in planning one's daily, weekly, monthly, or even annual life.

There are a number of journaling paths that can favor a parent with a child having special needs. It can go from infancy to dealing with kids to adulthood. Journals can also follow the path of thoughts, questions, and solutions. Here are three journals to explore: The three ways to keep a parenting journal are as follows:

(i) New baby journals
(ii) Parent/child journals
(iii) Personal question journals

- *(i) New baby journals:* If the child with special needs is an infant, maintaining a baby journal will help. Write down thoughts, observations, ideas, milestones, and educative points. The use of images and any piece of artwork that would perfectly convey thoughts and feelings are highly recommended. The ideas and solutions drafted can help in the search for problems in the future in case they arise.
- **(ii)** *Parent/child question journals:* A parent/child journal can be a journal in which the structure and content are put together by the parents and the siblings. This could be fun, as everyone would have an input. The sections might be much more than usual to accommodate the many things going on in the minds of each person, and the exercise can help strengthen the bond that exists between members of the family.

(iii) Personal question journals: This journal can be used for drafting ideas, thoughts, and points that encourage the search for answers. Here, whatever is written is structured in such a way that it provokes thoughts of the solution and seeks answers. This kind of journal is extremely good for stringing up difficult questions that have been left unanswered. Over time, answers to lingering questions would then be answered.

Journaling can help whoever is appointed to take care of the child with special needs after the parent is gone. The new caregiver would learn a number of things from the many writings of the parents. Also, the formulation of a journal will serve as a pleasant memory for the child with special needs. It can be something the child would hold on to in loving memory of the deceased parent.

A journal must not always be perfectly crafted, with scintillating thoughts and perfect grammar. The whole idea is to convey thought from the mind to paper. What is important is adequately doing so regardless of how lovely the method of doing so looks. Of course, there is no problem if the journal looks like a gorgeous piece of art. Just stay within the purpose of coming up with a journal and keep writing sincerely.

Notable Points

(i) *Carrying out individual assessments on your child would require both standardized and criterion-referenced tests.*

(ii) *Various tests include individual intelligence tests, group intelligence tests, skill evaluations, developmental and social history, observational records, and samples of student work.*

(iii) *Teachers require various measures to ensure that they get a clear understanding of your child's overall performance in relation to others at the same grade level.*

(iv) *Even though one-off evaluations that can measure a child's full range of assets and weaknesses are uncommon, assessments do give educators a sense of direction on how to give your child the best services.*
(v) *Journaling can serve as a source of information, documentation, and outlet for flow of emotions.*
(vi) *Journals can vary from new baby journals, parent/child journals, and personal question journals.*

Actionable steps

(i) *Write down which forms of assessment tests you have exposed your child with special needs to in the last year.*
(ii) *Write down areas of concern in their overall performance quotient.*
(iii) *Write down how journaling has helped you manage as a parent.*

- - -

Chapter 13
Before You Leave

In the previous chapter, we discussed issues relating to setting up the right modalities required for the optimum development of the child with special needs by the parent. It was established that the right environment carefully tailored to encourage spontaneous and continuous growth must be set up. Furthermore, the right education and support from within and outside the family circle and community ought to be sorted, as many forms of such support could help the child greatly.

But all the aforementioned, even though necessary to help the child with special needs grow and attain independence, are not enough in securing the future of the child. You, being a parent, have to go the extra mile to take other critical, legal actions that would directly affect your child upon your eventual demise.

(a) Special Needs Attorneys and Others

The need for an attorney cannot be overemphasized. Settling legal disputes between parents and the educational providers of their wards can be done without necessarily hiring an attorney, as ruled by the highest American court.

What Will Happen to my Special Needs Child When I am Gone

The U.S. Supreme Court ruled that parents and caregivers of children with special needs do not need to pay for legal services to litigate a school district over disputes that concern the educational needs of their children. The intricacies of the law would require a competent legal practitioner who knows the wherewithal of the struggles of the parents and child in terms of the interpretation of the law and helping advocate for their rights.

As a parent with a child with special needs, you may occasionally find yourself in peculiar situations that would necessitate going to court, thereby requiring the services of a special needs attorney. Regardless of what the case might be, an attorney who rightly fits the bill is crucial. Hiring the wrong attorney can result to you being fleeced, the attorney not pursuing the case as thoroughly as expected, and having little or no understanding or empathy for you, your child with disabilities, or the situation.

It is important that every parent or caregiver of a child with special needs find the right special needs attorney who would advocate for their family. Even though a lot of parents may not see the necessity for hiring a special needs attorney until they find themselves entangled in a situation requiring legal assistance, looking at the big picture, it becomes clear that having a special needs attorney at hand could eventually prove to be beneficial in the long run.

It is important for parents seeking the services of a special needs attorney to look out for certain qualifications. While it is true that all lawyers, regardless of their specialty, must have had comparable educational training in navigating the law, only a few would have gone on to qualify as special needs attorneys. So, while searching, you can look for an attorney that is seasoned in the knowledge of the laws of special education. This trait must be identified because the turf of special needs and special needs education has been proven to be quite intricate and complicated, so expertise is a compulsory trait to look out for.

Added to competence should be the search for experience. It is important to seek an attorney who has had many years of practice under their belt, particularly with special needs. There are more than a few capacities and cases in which an attorney ought to have sufficient experience when it comes to special needs. These areas should include simple negotiations and agreements, mediations, administrative and court hearings. There is no telling what a special needs parent would need at various points in time, which is why the need to have an attorney who has a vast experience in handling special needs cases remains a necessity.

An additional aspect to ponder when picking a special needs attorney is how sensitive they are to you, your child, and the case. A major red flag that should never be ignored is if the special needs attorney lacks the knowledge and sensitivity of your child's case or disability, making them unwilling to apply due diligence in the areas of research. If the compassion and understanding levels of the special needs attorney aren't satisfactory, it should be viewed as a total turn-off. The right attorney ought to appreciate the unique disability of your child and how it impacts your family. In the long run, if you do not feel assured with a particular attorney, the best action would be to seek a different one.

It is hard enough for you with a child having special needs to have a lot to deal with in general; pairing this up with a subpar attorney only makes the journey tougher. The idea here is to find an attorney of exceptional competence who is worth your complete trust and confidence.

(i) Estate Planning: An interesting fact in society today is that there are more people planning vacations and what cars to buy than there are people carrying out estate planning, which involves making deliberate decisions on who will come into their assets when they die. Admittedly, estate planning isn't as fun as scheduling a trip, but without the former, there would be no room for the owner of an estate to choose who gets what or everything that they worked so hard to earn.

Contrary to prevailing thoughts, estate planning is not an activity exclusively reserved for the wealthy. Without proper planning, settling one's dealings after they might have passed away could have a long-term impact on the loved ones left behind, even if the assets left behind are expensive, expansive, and invaluable. A mindset of not needing an estate plan could be easy to fall into, but here are a few points to consider that might change such a train of thinking so as to avoid possibly upsetting consequences for one's heirs.

(ii) It safeguards beneficiaries: Granted, there was a point in time when estate planning was well thought out to be an exercise that only people with high net worth did, but that has long changed. Currently, a lot of middle-class households do have to plan around and consider the possibility that their breadwinner(s) might unavoidably depart, and the little they left behind would have to be distributed amongst surviving household members. After all, not everyone has to be very rich to own something in the real estate or stock markets, both of which yield effects that would be worth passing on.

No matter what it is, from having a box of jewelry, owning a second home to possessing multimillion-dollar businesses, a person who eventually dies has no say or control over who would take control of what is left if estate planning isn't done before the eventuality of death.

This is so because the foremost element associated with estate planning is the designation of certain individuals as being heirs and/or coheirs to the assets of the deceased by the deceased themselves.

Typically, in an event where no estate plan was put in place, the courts would make the decisions on who gets what assets. This process is often undesirable and can linger for years; it can take sizable portions in the form of fees, and often ends up being messy. More often than not, the ruling would not take into account certain things, like whether or not a party is responsible, who should not be given unlimited access to cash and assets, and so on. Furthermore, the courts are in no position to spontaneously rule in favor of the surviving spouse, either.

(iii) It safeguards young children: The idea of death occurring at a young age can be unimaginable, but as a parent of young children, it is imperative for you to arrange for the inconceivable. This is where an aspect of estate planning called the will comes in.

It is important to name a guardian of your choice if you desire that your children be catered for following your desires especially if both parents pass away before their eighteenth birthday. Without such a will in place, the verdict of who gets to raise your children would be decided by the courts.

(iv) It saves beneficiaries from having to pay huge taxes: The general idea behind estate planning is to put up legal protection for all beneficiaries of the assets, which in some measures implies putting up legal protection from the Internal Revenue Service. This is done by transferring

allocated individual assets to inheritors with particular efforts toward reducing the amount of potential tax burden for them to the barest minimum.

With minimal effort put into estate planning, the testator significantly cuts down on a lot, or, in some cases, all of the federal and state estate inheritance taxes, the amount of which can run into large sums. Additionally, a number of ways can be adopted that would lessen the income tax which heirs might be compelled to pay. But without a plan, a lot of what is shared would end up with Uncle Sam.

(v) It eradicates family feuds: The death of a wealthy person can spark an unhealthy dispute, bitterness, and litigation that, if not managed properly, can linger for many years and ruin relationships. One sibling might feel more deserving of a bigger portion than the other; another might feel absolute control of the financial empire ought to be left to them, even though they are known to be undeserving. Such internal strife can prove to be very messy, with it ending in various litigations in court, which at worst can ultimately tear any family apart, or at best, leave scars that would take ages to heal.

One of the many advantages of having an estate plan is that it resolves battles even before they begin. With the testator formally choosing heirs who control what and how it is to be managed if they become cerebrally incapacitated, or after their demise, the testator formally and effectively crushes any impending family feud, going on to ensure that all assets are controlled in a fashion that they intended them to be.

In addition, an estate plan would also give a parent room to make tailored plans that were necessary, like drafting out provisions for a child with special needs or disabilities or setting up a trust for another who might not benefit in the long run from being given a lump sum. Again, an estate plan can assist a person in allocating more assets to the individual who dedicated their time and energy in nursing the testator in their later years, or in allocating less to one child for whom their educational expenses far superseded that of the other children.

An estate plan is crucial when it comes to establishing the sharing formula for all involved. The presence of more than one spouse or other children outside the immediate family makes it even more delicate and therefore shouldn't be ignored. The best remedy for protecting your assets and loved ones when you are no longer disposed to do so is to set up an estate plan.

(b) Setting up a Will

A will or testament can be described as a legal document that articulates a testator's wishes and desires as it relates to their estate (how it is to be distributed after they die). It also captures who in particular would stand as the executor of the will—one who would oversee the property until final dissemination is made. Properties whose devolution cannot be ascertained because a will or testament wasn't drafted would be disseminated, going by the concept of intestacy.

Historically, the terms "will" and "testament" have been used interchangeably, even though the predominant supposition back in the day was that a will differs from a testament in that the former referred exclusively to actual property, while the later referred exclusively to personal effects, but this is not the case today. As a result, the word "will" authentically captures both personal effects, as well as real property. However, a will might also fashion a testamentary trust that only comes into effect once the testator dies.

(i) Types of wills:

Generally, types of wills may include the following:

- *Nuncupative (inculpatory)* — also referred to as an oral or verbal will, it is a set of directives on the dissemination of one's assets given in the event that the testator is too ill or unable to effect a will in writing. In most jurisdictions, nuncupative wills are deemed illegal. Where they are legal, however, they necessitate a customary number of witnesses who are required to have written down what they witnessed as soon as they hear. This type of will is common with persons serving in the military and sailors.

- *Holographic will* — This will is typically handwritten, with the signature of the testator on the document. It is a common substitute for a will drafted by a lawyer. States that deem this type of will legally necessitates explicit requirements to prove its validity. The minimal requirements are evidence that the will was indeed drafted by the testator personally, confirmation that the testator was in a functional mental state, and the will has to capture the pattern of dissemination of the assets of the testator.

- *Self-proved* — This is a will that is crafted in a fashion that lets a probate court to, without difficulty, admit it as the accurate will of the testator. In some claims, for a will to be termed self-proving, two witnesses must give signatory under penalty of perjury that they indeed saw the testator imprint their signature and gave a vocal confirmation to them that it was their will. In the event that no one challenges the legitimacy of the will, the probate court then goes on to admit the will without hearing any testimony from the witnesses or other substantiation. Still, in other jurisdictions, an affidavit, signed by the testator and one or more witnesses and, in the presence of an attorney, openly attests that the will is unpretentious and that all official procedures that were followed must be presented.

- *Notarial*—This will is drafted by an attorney or notary and is typically drafted in the company of a witness, which the attorney provides. Under special circumstances, like when dealing with a testator who is visually impaired, an added witness is necessary. The will must be drafted in the most preferred language and must specify the date and domicile where it was drafted. Once prepared, the will must be read out to the testator and then signed by the same attorney and witness, in the presence of each other.

- *Mystic*—This will, also referred to as a closed, sealed, or secret will, is typically drafted and signed surreptitiously. The will is then presented to an attorney in public by the testator, accompanied by a written statement that further gives validity to the will. It is then signed by the attorney and witnesses present, who would later go on to testify before a court with their witnesses as evidence. Mystic wills do not have a large acceptance rate in most states in America. But where it is accepted, testimonies would have to either take the form of an affidavit effected after the demise of the testator or orally as deemed by the courts.

- *Reciprocal/husband and wife wills*—This will is exclusively designed to be adopted by life partners and couples who are legally married as a way of reassigning all of their assets to the living spouse or partner upon the demise of the other. Reciprocal wills are, for all intents and purposes, two distinct wills, which are then mirrored. On the other hand, reciprocal wills give allowances to each participating partner to tailor specific personal assets to beneficiaries of their choice, above and beyond the other spouse. Upon the demise of one spouse, and the eventual transfers to earlier named beneficiaries, the living spouse would then take possession of whatever is left of the deceased's estate. Again, in the event that the beneficiary named in the will dies, this kind of will permits the same allocated assets to pass to the children of the deceased or any of their surviving relatives.

- *Joint will*—This type of will combines two or more individuals' last wills, conjointly executing them as one. In a joint will, when one of the parties dies, the living party exclusively inherits the joint assets. If both parties die, the entire estate is transferred to their living children or relatives. It must be noted that a joint will is not the same as mutual wills, which comprise of reciprocal provisions that tie the dissemination of property reliant on the other.
- *Unsolemn will*—This type of will is described as one lacking the name of an executor. This is common with an affair in which there is something to protect.
- *Living will*—This will is drafted to legally communicate the wishes of an individual who is unable to speak for himself due to a tragic health condition or ordeal that must have left them

incapacitated. This type of will is crucial, as everyday dealings are so unpredictable.

A will enables the testator to regulate the exercise of rights of others over the estate they left behind. By drafting a will, some court costs and probate taxes linked with certification could be circumvented, as a result leaving more for the inheritors. Once the testator names an executor in the will, the executor would carry out the exclusive desires of the testator as touching the directives in the will. A testator can name a guardian for a minor or custodian for a person with special needs or disabilities in a will. This is referred to as a will trust, which can also be used as a tool for dissemination in a trust.

A will would necessitate the taking of inventory of the testator's possessions in a bid to effectively dispense it all among the beneficiaries. Assets belonging to the testator would typically comprise of any holdings bearing the name of the testator, business, joint ventures, trusts, or joint arrangements.

(ii) The functions of lawyers in the drafting of one's will:

Generally, there are no statutes or laws that insist that the drafting of a will be done exclusively by an attorney or a lawyer. However, individuals may seek the assistance and/or advice of a person with a background in law or legal matters to help them draft a will, use a software, fill a will form correctly, or simply draft their desires and wishes by themselves without any assistance. Still, some attorneys provide educational tutelage for people who desire to draft their own will.

But the fact remains that a will drafted by an attorney is often more thorough than one drafted by anyone else. First, an attorney is typically conversant with drafting such a document; therefore they can do so with minimal stress, errors, or avoidable mistakes that could put the part or all of a will in danger of becoming invalid. Furthermore, once a will is gotten from a lawyer, it generally emanates as being a slice of a total package of an estate plan that might comprise of other important provisions, like a living trust. Attorneys can go even further to tailor each will to meet the language and structure preferences of the testator.

Notable Points
(i) *Employing the services of an attorney can be exceedingly helpful.*
(ii) *When choosing an attorney, choose competence, experience, and passion for you and your child.*
(iii) *Estate planning is important in safeguarding all beneficiaries named in a will, protects the venerable, helps cut down on enormous taxes, and completely eliminates the likelihood of family feuds.*
(iv) *Although there is no legal obligation to hire an attorney to draft a will, it is better you do as they, through experience, know all that needs to be done.*

Actionable Steps
(i) *Write down what your recent efforts have been on estate planning.*
(ii) *Write down contacts of attorneys you might know for drafting your will.*
(iii) *Write down which type of will you desire to explore and why.*
(iv) *Research on your most preferred attorney and type of will.*

Chapter 14
Fundamentals of Crafting a Will

Upon the death of a testator, a last will lawfully approves the desires of the deceased to be committed for execution. Despite the fact that a great number of Americans affirm that a crucial aspect of having a comprehensive financial plan is to have a will. Many people still die without having drafted one, leaving their loved ones at the mercy of state laws and probate court. Ill-advisedly, many maintain the thought that they are rather too young to die and therefore have plenty of time. This ill-fated disposition always leads to putting off drafting a will until it is too late to do so.

According to data from several reputable government agencies in the U.S., about two and a half million people pass away annually in the U.S. alone. This is indicative of a death rate of about eight to a hundred individuals every year.

(a) Typical Composition of a Will

A will is composed of a number of items without which it would not be considered or admitted by a law court as being valid. And even though some things vary from one jurisdiction to the other, it must generally comprise the following:

- It must contain a publication, which is a conspicuous statement declaring that a will is being created and that the testator is the maker of the will. Generally, the words "last will and testament" offer such satisfaction on the face of the document.
- The testator must conspicuously state the revocation of wills and codicils previously written by them. If not, then the present will is in danger of being overruled by any previous will to the far-reaching extent to which both are inconsistent. On the other hand, a total show of inconsistency between two wills would imply that the earliest amongst them would be considered revoked.
- The testator may perhaps point out that they possess soundness of mind and have the aptitude to dispose of their assets. It should also be indicated that the testator does so willingly and without restrictions.
- The will must contain the date the document was created and the signature of the testator; these must be inputted by the company, no less than two fair-minded witnesses, who are individuals and who are not included as beneficiaries. Supernumerary (added witnesses) can be present in case of inquiries as to an interested-party conflict. Holographic wills normally do not require witnesses to authenticate the will. However, the testator's signature might need to be proven later on, depending on the jurisdiction.
- Witnesses who stand to be beneficiaries conspicuously named in the will may trigger either of the following:
    - outright disqualification from receiving anything under their will, or

- absolute invalidation of their status as being a witness.

In some jurisdictions, however, a beneficiary conspicuously named in the will becomes an improper witness as touching clauses that benefit him or her.

- The affixed signature of the testator must be placed at the very end of the Will as any subsequent writings after the signature would be ignored in its entirety. Furthermore, if the subsequent writings prove to be sensitive, capable of defeating the intentions of the testator, then it might lead to rendering the will invalid.
- One or more beneficiaries must be conspicuously named in the will; in some jurisdictions, however, a will maintains its validity if the will at hand revokes a standpoint in a previous one or designates an executor.

In public property jurisdictions, a will has no power to cut out a living spouse, who is entitled to a statutory minimum share of the testator's estate. Furthermore, a will cannot compel a beneficiary to commit crime, illegality, or immorality as a condition for receiving.

Still, in some claims, the children of the testator can be cut off from the will. In other claims, however, the least possible portion is fail-safe to living children with exceptions in particularly itemized situations. This is common and acceptable in a lot of civil law countries.

An inventory of the assets of a testator can generally include the following:

- Insurance
- Pensions/annuities
- Real properties/houses
- Funds

- Businesses/corporate interests
- Investments
- Lawsuits/settlement benefits
- Personal properties/effects

(b) Making Deliberate Provisions for Children with Special Needs and Disabilities

For a parent raising a child with special needs, it is possible that your child's challenges might not allow you to just sign off some large amount of funds to them to use how they see fit. This could prove to be very unwise, or even dangerous, putting them in a susceptible position. This is because some children with special needs or those with disabilities may not have the cognitive strength to manage their finances, which could lead to outright mismanagement of resources or abuse of the same.

There are a number of ways to manage such a challenge. You can explore the option of leaving your entire estate in the care of someone else whom you trust absolutely to oversee the dispensing of resources where necessary to look after your child with special needs. This option, however, is extremely risky, as an out-and-out gift implies that the estate lawfully belongs to the beneficiary, and unanticipated situations may come up, like death, obligations, and divorce, which could rapidly deplete all the resources, leaving your vulnerable child in a dire situation than before.

Even though this thought borders around a worst-case scenario, it does point out how things might turn around most unexpectedly, in spite of the best intentions of everyone. It is because of such unwanted occurrences that the option of ring-fencing the estate set aside for a child with special needs into a trust is best explored. This can be put in place in the standings of your will.

(c) Trust in Wills

You can create a trust in your will. These come in different shades and could be done in numerous ways as well. However, the most commonly used kind is a "disabled person's trust."

This type of trust is preplanned for a situation where the testator desires to leave part or all of their assets to a beneficiary who cannot safeguard and utilize the inheritance on their own. In these settings, you can put aside part of your assets in your will and commit them to chosen trustees who will oversee the management of the inheritance for the betterment of the beneficiary with disabilities for as long as they are still alive.

Furthermore, once the beneficiary with disabilities passes away, the trustees would then choose how and when to disseminate what is left of the trust to and amongst other prospective beneficiaries. This final stage can also be fully controlled by you as you can guide the trustees using an instrument referred to as a letter of wishes. The letter would clearly state how you would want the remainder of the trust to be channeled.

Putting up a disabled person's trust has a number of benefits that you can take advantage of:

- The assets contained within the trust do not belong to your child; this will help in ensuring that their availability does not disrupt their means-tested benefits.
- Even though the assets stay in the trust, they technically are owned by no one in their capacity. This will further secure the assets from being affected by any of the trustee's downward circumstantial

changes that may lead to the confiscation of their estate for debt settlement, divorce or death.
- Thanks to the trustees' discretions, which could generally be termed as unbiased and well-intentioned, your child will be better placed to benefit from the assets.
- Management of the contents of the trust will not be done by your child. So the fear of mismanagement would be greatly reduced.

(d) The Certification Process

The executor of the will must provide the following to fulfill conditions associated with the certification process. They include the following:

- Make available legally acceptable proof of the validity of the will.
- Offer a comprehensive inventory of all of the testator's assets that are intended to be disseminated according to the will.
- Inform all parties named in the will as beneficiaries.
- Inform all existing parties who are creditors of the estate.
- Inform any organizations or companies who are of interest in the estate.
- Evaluate all captured assets of the estate.
- Service all outstanding debts, taxes, fees, etc.
- Allocate the remaining assets following the wishes of the testator.

(e) Frequently Asked Questions about Estate Planning
- *What ensues if I die without writing a will?*

Passing away without a valid will renders you *intestate*. This implies that your entire estate would be sorted based on the prevailing laws of your state of residence, which outlines who comes into what. In the absence of any substantive executor named in the will or in the case where a will is declared invalid, a judge would appoint an *administrator* who would function in that capacity.

The designated administrator would typically be a neutral person, preferably a stranger to you or members of your household. Furthermore, the administrator would be bound by the probate laws of your state. By implication, the decisions that would be made by the administrator might not necessarily go along with your wishes and desires or those of your heirs.

- *Is employing an attorney to prepare my will necessary?*

While hiring a competent and experienced attorney who can deliver useful counsel on estate planning strategies could serve to your advantage, there aren't any laws that mandate this action. Hiring a lawyer is not required at all. Nevertheless, as long as your will meets the legal standard of writing a will in your state, it is binding, whether it was drafted by an attorney or not.

You can explore do-it-yourself templates online or find other options for will-writing guides at bookstores or libraries. The Department of Aging in states can also help in pointing you to resources for estate planning, which could be low cost or even free.

When you successfully draft out or update your will, it might also be a good time to ponder other advance planning instruments such as financial and health care powers of attorney to make sure that your desires are carried out even while you are still alive.

- *Is a joint will better than having separate wills?*

Even though your will, as compared to that of your spouse, could end up looking quite similar, distinct wills tend to make better sense. Furthermore, estate planners have long held a general disposition against joint wills, having little or no recognition in most states.

Separate wills give room for each spouse to add to anyone that they might feel should be included in their will, like ex-spouses, children from earlier relationships, etc.

- *Who qualifies to be a witness to a will?*

The witnesses to a will could be just about anyone, except those who have been named as beneficiaries of the will. This is done to avoid any possible conflict of interest. The witness must be termed *a disinterested witness*. Some states necessitate a minimum of two witnesses. In the event that an attorney drafts your will, then he cannot also function as a witness.

Your witnesses might have to sign what is referred to as a *self-proving affidavit* in the attendance of an attorney. Such an affidavit would hasten up the probate process, as in most cases, your witnesses would likely not be called into court by a judge to authenticate their signatures and the legitimacy of the will.

- *Whom should I write down as the executor of my will?*

Depending on how simple or complicated your life and will is, naming an executor might vary from your spouse, a grown-up child, to a dear friend or relative. However, the need to name an attorney as executor would be deemed wise if the nature of your estate is touchy and complex. You can also explore the option of naming joint executors, like your spouse and your attorney.

It is important to authorize your executor to handle all your outstanding payments and deal with any debts you might leave behind. Ensure that clear-cut words are used to address such issues, also giving flexibility to your executor to manage any associated issues that aren't explicitly stated in your will.

- *How do I leave particular items to particular beneficiaries?*

You can conspicuously spell out a particular personal property that you intend to leave to a particular heir in your will. Additionally, you can make an unconnected document referred to as a *letter of instruction* that you should keep alongside your will. A letter of instruction, although not validly binding in some states, is more informal than a will and can contain more details about the items and whom it should go to. You can also input additional data about any amount of things that will assist your executor to resolve your estate; like account numbers, passwords, and even instructions on your burial.

- *Which is the safest place to store my will?*

Since the probate court would typically request your original will before commencing any processing of your estate, it is important to keep the document safe and yet reachable. Do not be overzealous in hiding it as it must be located in the event of your passing for its content to be properly executed. If you choose to put it away in a bank, then you must ensure that your family will easily have access to it when you die. Better still, if you can keep it safely at home within a waterproof and fireproof safe to prevent the total loss of the document through natural disasters like fire or flood, it is imperative that you keep a copy with your attorney or an individual you are confident in. Such copies duly signed by you can be used to establish your plans. The nonappearance of an original copy, however, can make matters difficult, without which there is no assurance that your estate will be established as you had desired.

- *How frequently do I have to update my will?*

The only will that stands out to be used is the most recent one that exists at the moment of your demise. Updating your will is dependent on you. Some people never update theirs, while others do so regularly. It is recommended that major life changes should prompt you to revisit and update your will. Instances like matrimony, divorce, and childbirth, the demise of an heir or executor, an important acquisition or legacy, and the like should not be overlooked. Also, maybe you named a guardian for your kids, but now they are all grown; this means you would have to update your will by removing guardianship completely, except for kids with special needs or disabilities. Reviewing your will every two or three years can be a good period to keep in mind.

- *Does anyone have the right to challenge my will?*

Challenging a will is meant to test the legal validity of all or portions of the deed. A beneficiary who feels affronted by the expression of a will might elect to contest it. A spouse, ex-partner, or child who is confident that your itemized desires are in contradiction of local probate laws might elect to contest the will.

A will can be contested for any number of whys and wherefores:

- It was not witnessed appropriately.
- Your soundness of mind was in doubt as and when you signed it.
- It is the product of compulsion or scam.

The path toward a successful contest of a will is to locate valid legal errors within it. So, a drafted and truly executed will is the best guard.

Chapter 15
Letter of Intent and Care Plan

(a) Letter Of Intent

Drafting a letter of intent (LOI) to your child with special needs or disabilities can aid in giving them family permanence and ease after you might have passed away. One of the most prized assets your child possesses is you and your ability to cater to them without holding back. You, unlike anyone else, completely recognize the gradations that could be attributed to the coping mechanisms of your child and what can elicit unpleasant results.

An LOI has the sole purpose of conveying these comprehensive traits alongside real-world specifics about your child's life so that once you are no longer available, a different family member or caregiver would be able to make sound choices as touching the care of your child. An LOI is not to be thought of as something meant for aged parents; it is recommended that parents, no matter how young or old, who cater to children with special needs should have an LOI. Furthermore, this letter should be reviewed every year, updating its contents where applicable. Also, misfortunes and ailments that may come about are as rampant a need to have an LOI as is your ultimate demise.

Even though an LOI is not a legally binding document, it is widely regarded as being one document of utmost importance that any parent can formulate for the imminent well-being of their child with special needs. This letter is central in your child's special needs plan as it offers your unique perspective as touching the specifics of their life. Drafting an LOI is not as hard as many think it to be; there are tons of templates available on the web, and other formats and ideas could be gotten from books and libraries.

It is important not to lose the soul of an LOI; the letter is meant to chaperone a guardian, family member, or caregiver designated to give care to your dependent child. You will need to sift through outlooks and anticipations, identifying people, dwellings, and services that relate to your child with special needs. It is recommended that you take out some time, say a week, to monitor your child, take notes each day as you work together with your child, thinking through some of the far-reaching subjects, keeping a record of how you may feel about your child and their imminent future.

An LOI may contain a written address to anyone you may desire; terms like, "To Whom It May Concern," or "To my Guardian(s) and/or Trustee(s)" are commonly used and are appropriate. There are a few areas that the LOI should cover. They include:

- *Your family background:* This should include your date and place of birth, your upbringing, and marriage; it should also capture short narrations about your family members and other kinsfolk or special friends.
- *General overview of your child:* This is a passing summary of the life of your child to the current period

and your overall contemplations and anticipations about your child's future. Also, a brief narrative of the birth of your child and their relations to particular family members or friends would greatly compliment your description of fond memories about your child.

- *Your child's daily calendar:* It is possible for prospective caregivers to fail to make out varying functionality that your child may have as compared to their previous experiences. It is therefore, essential to take account of a list of daily habits, preferred activities, and events or tasks that might be repulsive to them. Also, it is important if you can mention in the letter if your child can help with household tasks such as doing the dishes; such activities are recommended as a child's self-esteem is greatly enhanced simply by their contributions to even the most ordinary facets of family life. However, if your child loves one activity while another irritates them, it is important to make this known to the prospective caregivers.

- *Your child's dietary regime:* Including your child's dieting regime is important. List out their preferred foods and any particular way in which the food ought to be made or served. Listing out foods that your child does not like, is allergic, to or must never be given owing to counterproductivity due to medication is also important.

- *Your child's medical care:* There is a need for a detailed description of your child's medical history, disabilities, allergies, current pediatricians, therapists, and hospitals. Also, clearly outline your child's medical and therapeutic routines, appointments, and goals of each session. Furthermore, outline present medications, alongside their mode of administration and the purpose for which they are being taken. If any medication should be avoided or that has not worked as effectively for your child, they too must be mentioned in the letter.

- *Your child's education:* The letter should contain details about your child's educational involvement. Also, do outline your aspirations for your child's imminent education, comprising regular and special lessons, specific schools, associated services, mainstreaming, supplementary activities, and leisure. Outline your desires as per the kinds of educational emphasis to be deployed; from vocational and academic to overall communication. Mention any particular packages, tutors, or interrelated service providers that you may have a preference for in pursuit of your child's overall life plan.

- *Your child's welfares received:* Clearly state all the types of governmental aids your child received in the past, is currently receiving, and which he might be eligible to receive in the coming days or months. This may comprise Medicare, SSI/SSDI, Medicaid, food stamps (Supplemental Nutritional Assistance Program), and housing support. Provide the contact information of the agencies, your child's case(s) ID numbers, the recertification route for each aid, alongside other important information like dates and other requirements.

- *Your child's employment:* Outline in the letter a detailed description of the work and environments your child may enjoy. Indicate if they prefer open employment backed by supervision, a cozy workshop, or an activity epicenter. You can also list any firms that, to the best of your knowledge, provide such kind of employment and thus might be of particular interest to your child.

- *Your child's residential environment:* It is important to outline the living arrangements of your child with family members, friends, or other shelters. If your child will no longer be able to keep living with these people once you seize to be their primary caregiver, then it becomes important to write in the letter the best options you would have the guardian consider. You can clarify whether or not you fancy your child living in an institute or group home, if your choice of a home should be within the same community he is being raised in, and the like.
- *Your child's social environment:* Let the letter contain the kinds of social undertakings that your child loves to engage in: things like sports, building sandcastles, dancing, or watching movies. Specify if there is a need to be dispensing cash allowances to your child and how frequently it ought to be done. Finally, point out if taking vacations and travels are part of what your child enjoys doing and how frequently should such be done and with whom.
- *Your child's religious environment:* You can also go on to indicate your child's religion and any preferred place of worship you would want them attending. Outline the names of all local clergy that may be at ease with your child and family. Give a detailed description of the religious education of your child, indicating whether or not your child has found them interesting.
- *Your child's behavior management:* If there are any behavioral management programs in which your child is being enrolled at the moment, it is important to state those in the letter, alongside any programs that you have planned out for him to attend in the future. Indicate the level of impact these programs are having and whether or not the child finds them interesting.

- *Your child's final rites arrangements:* You can write down your wishes for your child's final arrangements when he eventually passes on. If you have a funeral planned out, or you desire a cremation, the choice of cemetery, putting up a monument, holding a pious service, and all such wishes can be captured in great detail.
- *Other relevant information:* You may also add in any additional information that you consider to be of tremendous importance, which would offer the best assistance to whoever would take on the responsibility of catering for your child.

As soon as the LOI is drafted, signed, and dated appropriately, efforts must be put in place to carry out an annual review of the document, updating part or all of it if necessary. In addition, you should inform your child's prospective caregiver of the existence of such a letter and where to access it upon your demise. Going about reviewing the document annually alongside the prospective caregiver could even be a better option than simply informing them of the existence of such a letter. The letter should be safeguarded alongside other pertinent legal and private documents that pertain to your child.

It is noteworthy to mention that the LOI can trigger some very strong emotions when being written, as it can serve as your first glimpse of the future of your child without you being there by their side. Nevertheless, as soon as it is finished, it would mark an important milestone reached toward crafting a comprehensive road map for prospective trustees and caregivers. Being a parent responsible for the nurturing of a child with special needs, you can find solace in the fact that you are making sure the utmost quality of life is being offered for your child simply by setting the foundation for as unbroken an alteration as possible long after you pass.

(b) Care Plan

A care plan can be described as a compilation of medical details regarding your child for the purpose of sharing it with others. It is a piece of drafted information concerning how best to manage the health of your child. Typically, the care plan is developed by the child's doctor and parent or caregiver.

Generally, a care plan would include but would not be limited to the following key points:

- A description of all medicines your child is currently taking and the times for their administration.
- A detailed description of foods that should never be given to your child, maybe due to allergies or reactions with medications.
- A detailed description of how frequently your child gets physical therapy.
- A detailed description of what to do for your child when they are in a state of emergency.

(c) Why Develop a Care Plan?

Preparing a care plan can serve as a tool in the hands of anyone who is saddled with catering for your child with special needs, either for a season or as a named guardian or caregiver when you are no longer alive to do so yourself. This may comprise of nurses, doctors, teachers, therapists, childcare providers, emergency medics, relief providers, blood relatives, supports, and neighbors.

Furthermore, a care plan can come in handy for families in several ways, which may include:

- If you choose to hand over a two-page care plan about your child with special needs to medics, counselors, dentists, tutors, childcare providers, and visiting family and friends, it can serve as a "getting everyone on the same page" note that could greatly help each person deal with the child more appropriately. You can even go on to attach a lovely picture of your child to the document.

- Keeping a care plan close by can help in times of emergency, when there is a crisis, or if the child is simply having a bad day. Important information contained in the plan can assist any health care provider who attends to the child.

- In the event that you choose to draft an LOI, the information in the care plan would come in handy in adding it into the letter to help the prospective caregiver know exactly how to manage the child in the event of a medical crisis.

Notable Points

(i) *An LOI is intended to clearly outline all that needs to be known about your child to Whom It May Concern for the purpose of adequately catering for them when you are no longer available to do so.*

(ii) *Your typical LOI should capture the following: family background, general overview of your child, child's daily calendar, dietary regime, medical care, and education.*

(iii) *It should also capture your child's welfares received, employment, residential, social, and religious environment. In addition, the behavior management, final rites arrangements and other relevant info about your child should all be included.*

(iv) A care plan is your child's medical history and all relevant information concerning their health that might help a prospective caregiver.
(v) A carefully formulated care plan can help people working around your child to do so with requisite knowledge.
(vi) It will help in times of emergency.

Actionable steps
(i) Write down what you know about an LOI and a care plan.
(ii) Research further on the subjects and speak to your attorney for guidance.
(iii) Plan to draft out an LOI.
(iv) Plan to draft out a care plan.

– – –

Chapter 16
Special Needs Trust, Life Insurance

A special needs trust, also referred to as a supplemental needs trust, can be described as a particular kind of unchangeable trust that subsists under common law that permits heirs with special needs or disabilities to relish the use of assets held in the trust, particularly for their assistance, while simultaneously letting the heir get critical needs-based government support. Quite a lot of common law countries have established tailored bills related to the design and implementation of special needs trusts. And where such bills do exist, then the validity of any special needs trust would be subject to requirements itemized in the bill. In America, many states have long-established bills.

In general, unchangeable trusts are employed for the protection of assets belonging to minors, heirs with disabilities or special needs or simply as a means of protecting assets. Such a trust is also used to clench and manage assets proposed for the assistance of the receiver, particularly if the receiver has no capacity to manage their fiscal affairs. Special needs trusts can also serve as asset pools, letting otherwise disabled people still meet the requirements for governmental aid.

Special needs trusts can offer remuneration to, and safeguard the resources of, minors and individuals with physical or mental challenges. They are often used to accept an inheritance or proceeds from injury settlements for a minor or a person with special needs or disability or are established from the income of reparation for illegal injuries, legal action, or insurance payments. Typically, a character of trust is that their eventual management might be in the hands of either a family member (in the case of a private trust) or by trustees allotted by the court. Where a trust is set up for a child or young individual with special needs or disability, caution is exercised in choosing suitable trustees to oversee the assets and to handle imminent auxiliary appointments.

Special needs trusts are typically established under the supervision of an organized estate planner in collaboration with an experienced legal and fiscal team just to make certain that the trust is established correctly. Again, approved nonprofit establishments are commonly allowed to oversee a special needs trust program. Such mutual trusts are accessible all over the United States and are every so often focused on disabilities.

(a) Guidelines for Opening a Special Needs Trust

Here are a few recommendations:

- *Comprehending the need for a trust:* A special needs trust lets you put some monies aside for the imminent care of your child living with special needs or disabilities while simultaneously guarding the SSI and Medicaid that are important for the provision of essential medical and income support.

Looking closely at the requirements for qualifying for such government benefits, the individual must have no more than $2,000 in cash assets. The introduction of a financial gift, reimbursement, or legacy amount would revoke these benefits, leaving the individual with monies they cannot manage themselves and, in all probability, not having a sufficient amount of money to care for themselves throughout their lives.

- *Figure out the best category to explore:* Trusts come in two categories: either the revocable or irrevocable trust. For the revocable trust, you can alter its terms and contents or even choose to terminate it during your lifetime. This cannot be done to an irrevocable trust. Unless you are extremely wealthy, a revocable trust is always recommended even by legal professionals.

    For individuals who have a large estate, establishing an irrevocable trust can help safeguard against humongous estate taxes, which are taxes the federal government and states specify on the type of irrevocable trust that exists under common law charge on assets when they are moved from a testator to beneficiaries. By law, assets in an irrevocable trust are commonly not tallied as being part of a taxable estate.

    As of 2019, federal estate taxes apply exclusively to assets worth more than $11.4 million per person or $22.8 million per couple. Even though these figures change annually owing to inflation, the federal tax hardly affects smaller estates.

- *Pick the right kind of trust too:* Special needs trusts are typically financed by a third party, which is usually a parent or grandparent and can be harmonized with the family's entire estate plan. The trust clenches funds or assets that you set aside for the receiver's benefit.

On the other hand, pooled disability trusts are self-funded by individuals with a disability, usually from a personal injury grant or legacy. A typically pooled trust program is usually set up and overseen by a nonprofit corporation; additionally, such trusts have to be established in the same period when the funds were received.

Funds from both types of trusts can be used to purchase mobility equipment, dental and optic services, hearing aids, special education, recreation and travel, transport, equipment, and clothing.

- *Seeking the help of a professional:* Experienced estate planners and fiscal and case managers can help with a fresh viewpoint on the best moves to take to avoid 'what if' scenarios. Because guidelines surrounding trusts can be complex and ever changing, it is imperative to choose an attorney or nonprofit that focuses on these types of trusts.

- *Carefully select a trustee:* All forms of trusts necessitate the designation of a trustee. The trustee oversees the funds in the trust and approves the disbursements of funds exclusively for the sole benefit of the heir. The trustee is also in charge of reporting to agencies providing assistance and staying in touch with fluctuating codes of practice.

(b) *Life Insurance*

Life insurance, sometimes referred to as life assurance, can be described as an agreement entered into by an insurer or assurer or an insurance policyholder. The insurer agrees to pay the named beneficiary an amount of money referred to as a benefit if the insurance policyholder dies. In exchange, the insurance policyholder pays a premium. Conditions in the contract may trigger payments once a life-threatening illness gets in view. Depending on what you stated in the contract, payments of the agreed premium are commonly regular or lump sum. Other payments, however, like funeral costs, can be incorporated into the benefits.

Life policies are legally binding, and the limitations of the insured happenings are clearly stated in the terms of the contract. However, to limit the legal responsibility of the insurer, unambiguous exclusions are usually inputted into the contract; claims connected to fraud, civil turmoil, suicide, war, or riot are common instances for omission.

Today, contemporary life insurance has been expanded to capture retirement products like annuities and products in the asset management industry.

Life-based contracts can be categorized into the following:

- *Protection policy:* This policy is intended to offer a lump sum reimbursement if a stated incident occurs. This has become a very common form of protection policy insurance over the years.
- *Investment policy:* This policy is targeted at growing capital through steady or distinct premiums. In the U.S., popular forms include universal life, whole life, and variable life policies.

With a robust life insurance, you can set up a safe fiscal cushion that would see to the care of your loved ones once you die. A life insurance policy can take the pressure off of dealing with the abrupt fiscal repercussions of a person's demise, mainly if the departed was the breadwinner of the household.

The issue with this, however, is that without necessary precautions, the lump sum disbursements might be subject to 40 percent legacy tax. This implies that almost 50 percent of the reserves you so devotedly saved could be lost.

(c) Should You Put Your Life Insurance into a Trust?

Putting your life insurance into a trust has become a prevalent preference for solving this problem. By doing so, the funds would not be part of your estate, removing its liability for inheritance tax.

Taking this step is a resolution that ought to be taken very seriously as it is typically irrevocable. It is therefore wise to ensure that you understand all the long-term inferences. This could be done by engaging an experienced fiscal advisor before making such comprehensive decisions.

(i) The pros of having life insurance in a trust:
- Prompt payment of your assets out to your named beneficiaries.
- No part of the proceeds would be captured on your entire estate in the event of your death. This aids in liability reduction when it comes to paying inheritance tax.
- It is a further safeguard at ensuring that your life insurance payouts end up going directly to your named beneficiaries.

(ii) The cons of holding life insurance in a trust:
- This decision is practically irrevocable. The moment your life insurance is secured within a trust, you will not be able to take it back out.
- By placing your life insurance policy into a trust, you consequently give up complete control over it.

(d) Writing Your Life Insurance Policy in Trust

Life insurance placed into a trust can be described as a legally binding agreement, wherein you give authority to a trustee to make sure the proceeds from your life insurance policy are expended according to your wishes and desires. If the overall value of your estate is estimated to be above $11.5 million, then it would be subject to a 40 percent inheritance tax. So life insurance written into a trust could be a way out to secure your hard-earned money.

(e) Acquiring a Life Insurance Trust Deed

Putting life insurance into a trust can be done by first creating a trust deed. This is a legal document that summarizes the parties that comprise the trust, the terms of the trust, and the beneficiaries of the trust. A trust deed can be described as a legal assurance that makes sure your life insurance benefit is used precisely as intended. It functions as a will for the funds retained within the trust. This, by implication, removes the necessity for probate. This does not serve as a substitute for the will that captures the rest of your estate. Receiving a life insurance trust deed is a legal procedure that ratifies the authority of the trust to deal with your life insurance benefit when you pass away.

(f) The Dynamics of Life Insurance

Typically, life insurance policies may have two key components, which includes a death benefit and a premium.

- *The settler or donor*: This is referring to you, or whomever it is that is assigning their assets into a trust.
- *Trustee*: This is the individual or person who is legally chosen to manage the assets in a trust. Typically, the trustee is well known to and a confidant of the settler. It is also important to choose a trustee who is, by all ramifications, likely to live longer than you.

- *Beneficiary*: This refers to anyone whom you named that would receive the proceeds of trust upon your eventual death.
- *Death benefit:* The death benefit, also called the face value, is the total cash that the insurer promises to the named legatees in the event of the death of the insured. The insured could, for instance, be you, the parent, while the beneficiary could be your child with special needs. You would then pick the preferred death benefit aggregate going by the projected imminent needs of the receiver. The insurer would then decide whether or not an insurable interest will accrue and if the prospective client meets the requirements for the coverage going by the insurer's requirements as it interrelates to time of life, well-being, and the proximity of the insured to any hazardous activities.
- *Premiums:* Premiums are the funds that the insurer pays for insurance. At the death of the insured, the insurer is obligated to pay the death benefit, and payment of the premium is determined partially by the likelihood of the insurer paying to go by the life expectancy of the insured. The duration of life, sex, medical history, work-related hazards, and high-risk hobbies of the insured are some of the factors that impact life expectancy. Furthermore, the insurer's operating expenses are deducted from the premium. The size of a premium depends on how large the death benefits are, the height of individual risks, and the permanent policies that amass cash worth.
- *Cash worth:* Typically, permanent life insurance comes with cash worth, which serves dual purposes. First, the savings account, which houses funds amassed on a tax-deferred basis, is used by the policyholder during the life of the insured. Some policies, however, may place

limitations on withdrawals, subject to fund usage. For instance, the policyholder might decide to take out a loan in contradiction of the policy's cash worth, having to pay interest. The cash value is an active benefit that stays with the insurer when the insured passes on. Therefore, any unsettled loans against the cash worth will lessen the policy's death benefit.

Putting your life insurance into a trust would mean selecting trustees, getting an insurance provider, and deciding on whether or not you desire to place life insurance into a trust straightaway or allocate it to the trust at a later period. It is imperative that you make a well-informed decision about whether or not to place your life insurance into a trust.

(g) Who Should Buy Life Insurance?

Here are some instances of individuals who ought to buy life insurance:

- *Parents/guardians of minor children:* It is common for the death of a parent who is a primary caregiver to minors to plunge the latter into deep financial hardship. Buying life insurance can ensure the financial security of the children up until they grow and can look after themselves.

- *Parents/caregivers with adult children having special needs:* Life insurance can help secure funds for the imminent care of children who need permanent care, who will never be self-sufficient when their parents or caregivers die. The death benefits can be channeled to support a special needs trust, to be managed by a fiduciary for the benefit of the adult child.

- *Adults who own property together:* Couples married or not, have obligations together; paying bills, servicing loans, and the like. This means that the death of one of the spouses could turn out to be extremely disastrous to the other, financially. A life insurance policy can help secure the future of a living couple and help ease the financial burden of the same.

- *Aged parents who desire to leave funds to their caregiver adult children:* It is common for some children to sacrifice their time to care for their aged parent who needs it. Still others offer their help through direct fiscal support. Through life insurance, the parent can offer some kind of reimbursement to their adult child once the parent dies.
- *Young adults whose parents acquired and cosigned a private student loan:* A parent can enter serious financial difficulty once their child passes away for whom they once acquired a student loan. So what could be done is for the adult child to buy life insurance that can guarantee a benefit for the parent upon the unexpected death of the former.
- *Married pensioners:* Pensioners can pick their full pension, going on to buy life insurance to benefit their partner as against having to choose between a pension payout that proposes a spousal benefit and one that doesn't.

(h) Using Life Insurance for Planning the Future of Your Child with Special Needs

Here are a few tips that can help you plan the future for your child with special needs:

- It is important to have adequate long-term care insurance and individual disability insurance for yourself. This is because eventually becoming disabled or in need of long-term care can complicate things for the family.

- To finance your child's lifetime needs, it is imperative that you capitalize on a whole life insurance policy. This type of life insurance also offers cash value, which you can lend when there are any emergencies.
- You should also explore the options of significant riders, like a waiver of premium. This rider will ensure that your premium is paid if you become disabled. Another significant rider is the guaranteed insurability rider; this would enable you to buy more life insurance in the future without necessarily submitting yourself to a medical exam.
- Following the stipulated laws in your state, it is important that you not only choose a legal guardianship but also ensure that you pinpoint a substitute or reserve guardian for your child with special needs. This would guarantee continuity of life peradventure things do not go as planned with the named primary guardian.
- Make sure that your named backup guardian is not a novice when it comes to the management of funds and benefits of the child; that should include Medicare and SSI.

(i) **Kinds of Life Insurance**

Many different types of life insurance are available to meet all sorts of needs and preferences.

- *Term Life:* This kind of insurance is valid for only a stipulated number of years, which then brings it to a close. Typically, terms range from ten, twenty, or thirty years.
- *Level Term:* This kind of insurance is one in which the same premiums are paid each year.
- *Increasing Term:* This kind of insurance is one wherein premiums are increasing as the insured ages.

- *Permanent:* This kind of insurance is valid for the entire duration of the insurer's life. Furthermore, this kind of insurance is generally more costly compared to other terms.
- *Single-Premium:* This kind of insurance ensures that all of the premiums due to be paid by the policyholder are paid in a lump sum and at once, instead of making those payments every month, quarter, or year.
- *Whole Life:* This is a kind of permanent life insurance with the unique characteristic of amassing cash value.
- *Universal Life:* This also is a kind of permanent life insurance with a unique characteristic cash value component that receives interest over time. In terms of premium payments, universal life insurance can be as good as life insurance. Also, the premiums and death benefits can be altered as time goes on.
- *Guaranteed Universal*: This is a kind of universal life insurance that has no capacity to build cash value. It is generally a low premium plan compared to whole life.
- *Variable Universal:* This is a kind of insurance term that gives the insured the liberty to invest the cash value. However, various terms and conditions would be put in place to protect the liquidity of the insurer.
- *Indexed Universal:* This is a kind of universal life insurance that allows the insured to receive a stationary or equity-indexed rate yield on the cash value component.
- *Burial or Final Expense:* This is a kind of permanent life insurance with a meager death benefit. Despite the benefit not being tangible, beneficiaries are at liberty to dispense it as desired.

- *Guaranteed Issue:* This is also a kind of permanent life insurance that is generally accessible to individuals with medical challenges that somewhat renders them uninsurable. The term is such that no payments are made as a benefit for the first two years the policy is in force because of the volatility risk of the insured person. This is with the exception that the cause of death is accidental in nature. On the other hand, the policy premiums alongside its corresponding interest would be returned to the beneficiaries by the insurer in the event that the insured passes away during that period.

Notable Points

(i) Trusts are formulated to simply protect assets—the assets of minors and heirs with disabilities or special needs.

(ii) To set up a trust, you have to understand why you may need a trust, find the best type for you, and select the right kind after hearing from a professional.

(iii) Choosing a trustee can be tricky; so be careful.

(iv) A life insurance is an agreement in which an insurer agrees to pay the named beneficiary a benefit if the insurance policyholder dies.

(v) Insurance could either be a protection policy or an investment policy.

(vi) Putting life insurance into a trust can be done by first creating a trust deed.

(vii) There are various types of insurances. Ensure you choose the best that would suit you and your child with special needs.

Actionable Steps

(i) Write down all the trusts you have formulated.

(ii) Write down insurances that you hold.

Start working on doing them if you have not.

Chapter 17
Estate Planning - Quick Summary

Eleven Things to Do Before You Pass Away

People rarely ever want to ponder their mortality, as it is not a pleasant thought. Nevertheless, getting your businesses in order is extremely necessary for everyone. It is a fact that anyone with decent assets stands to gain from estate planning, which incorporates more than simply drafting out writing a will. Here is a quick summary of all you have to do before you pass away in a bid to secure the future of your child with special needs.

- *Collect contact info and vital documents:* Documents such as vehicle titles, property deeds, official birth and marriage certificates, your attorney's contact info, those of your insurance broker, doctor, and the like should be collected and kept in a safe, dry place. Keeping them safe should be an exercise done with the predisposition that they should be easy to access by your family or trusted ones in the event where you are no longer alive to do so. Also, the compilation of all sensitive documents can help immensely when you begin planning your estate.

- *Complete the last will and testament:* A will is one of the most significant estate planning documents you could ever draft. It captures all your wishes and desires as touching how you want your entire assets disseminated, to which beneficiaries, and in what instances. Unless you draft out a will, you will be leaving everything you own in the hands of the state's intestacy laws, which might not go in the direction that you desire.
- *Complete the advance directive:* An advance directive can be described as a legally binding document in which you indicate the name and contact info of an individual who would, in the case of a medical emergency, authorize your most preferred medical treatment should you experience incapacitation or are otherwise not capable of stating your preferences yourself.

  Common items spoken about in advance directives consist of breathing and feeding tubes, life support, home treatments, and other life-preserving remedial treatments.
- *Initiate a power of attorney:* The power of attorney lets you publish the name and contact info of a trusted individual who will be responsible for making decisions on your behalf in case you experience incapacitation. The power of attorney may be tailored to best serve your domestic, medical, or financial interests.

  An attorney's health care power is similar to an advance directive. Furthermore, to enable others to interact with medical professionals about you, you would need to prepare a Health Insurance Portability and Accountability Act.

- *Create a living trust:* As discussed earlier, with a living trust, you get to safeguard your wishes and decisions as to how your assets will be disseminated, fast-track disbursement of funds to beneficiaries, and protect their inheritance from excessive taxes.

    As the grantor, you tentatively maintain control over all properties placed within the trust for as long as you live. Upon your demise, however, your preselected trustee would then manage the trust, going on to disburse your assets, following your directives. This would go on without any intervention from probate, which could potentially save both time and money.

- *Apprise your beneficiaries:* In the event that you have retirement accounts, life insurance, pensions, transfer-on-death, or pay-on-death (POD) accounts, then you need to update your beneficiaries. Any changes to your family status should call for an immediate review of your beneficiaries.

- *Safeguard your digital assets:* Your digital presence, if any, must be properly managed in the event of your death. Other things to handle could include your online investment, bank, and shopping accounts. Social media apps like Facebook, for example, provide a section where you can choose someone to take control of your account once you die. Additionally, decide on what would happen with blogs, websites, and any other online platform on which you are active.

- *Plot your final arrangements:* If you desire certain things done after you die, such as organ donation or particular funeral rights, alongside provisions for

their eventual payments, accounts such as POD bank accounts do serve the perfect purpose of managing funeral expenses. It is not recommended that you place such demands within your will, as wills are rarely read immediately. As an alternative, a letter to your estate administrator or loved ones is good enough.
- *Create and store copies:* After you successfully collect all your relevant documents and create your will and other kinds of trusts and insurances, it is important to make copies and store the originals in a safe place. Ensure that at least one person you trust will be able to reach these documents after your demise.
- *Have an open conversation with your loved ones:* You can take the time to sit with your loved ones and discuss your plans and wishes together. Making your desires clear could prove to be critical when it comes to following them to the letter. It would further eliminate any doubts, guesses, or fears they might have. Such a conversation does not have to be gloomy. Again, you can take the time to chat about priceless memories, passing along memorable pictures and stories.
- *Stay current on everything:* It is not enough to simply put together your estate plan and stack them in that safe. You have to revisit those important documents at least once a year to update them where necessary in line with your intentions.
- *Designate a guardian for your child: Guardian of minor:* It is imperative for you as a parent of a child(ren) who is under age eighteen to designate a

legal guardian who will cater to them in the event that you die before the children enter adulthood.

- *Guardian Advocate:* On the other hand, your child with special needs would require a guardian to cater to them, to fare their finances, and make medical choices on their behalf even after growing up and legally becoming adults in the eyes of the law. Within your estate planning documents, you can appoint replacement guardians for your adult children with disabilities, just as you would if the child were still young and under the age of eighteen. On the other hand, you can assign a standby guardian who will immediately step in once the designated guardian also passes on, or you can give the court authorization to appoint a coguardian to simultaneously cater to your child. If you choose to explore this option, the surviving guardian will, therefore, continue to function as the sole guardian upon the demise of one of the guardians.

- *Ensure your child applies for SSI benefits before age twenty-two:* Indeed, your child with special needs might not qualify for SSI if they are younger than age eighteen. This is because to determine the eligibility of your child, social security administration (SSA) will look at your earnings and assets as the parent. Once your child with special needs turns eighteen, however, SSA will then look exclusively at the income of your child in determining their eligibility for SSI. When a person is considered disabled by the SSA earlier than age twenty-two, the child with disabilities would be qualified to get SSDI off of your pay record once you become incapacitated or die.

SSDI benefits can be considerably greater than SSI benefits, which as of 2012 was capped at $698 per month for qualified individuals.

Actionable Steps

(i) *Review your existing preparedness to potential misfortune or demise.*

(ii) *Evaluate your financial security and the safety of its transmission to your wards when you pass away.*

(iii) *Review your efforts toward securing the future of your child with special needs as far as your will is concerned.*

(iv) *Review your efforts in setting up your child with special needs in getting maximum government benefits.*

Review your choice of guardianship.

– – –

Chapter 18
When You Are Gone

The day of your death will eventually come, and your family and loved ones will have to deal with it, no matter how much they wish circumstances were different. It is a fact that you all must get comfortable with.

By putting effort toward adequate planning, you do a huge kindness to your family members, particularly your children with special needs. While you are here, you must do the needful, talking to your wards about the subject of death and the inevitability of you passing in the future. This would prepare them for how to ultimately handle the event when the time comes.

Furthermore, it is expected that you would have arranged for your child with special needs to have had the fundamentals of robust living before your exit. You have to surround your child with the right environment, provide the right education, enlist them in the right health care, and elicit the right support. All these would help them be more comfortable while you are around, and in due course, they would make the most of life after you are gone.

Other important steps that you ought to take would be to have your family, particularly your child with special needs, covered legally as far as your estate is concerned. Putting up a will, setting up a trust, drafting up an LOI, and setting up relevant life insurance programs are some of the things that could make a difference in your child's life when you pass.

In this chapter, we would consider measures that you can put in place that would help protect your child with special needs when you are gone. These measures would ensure that your child's rights are strictly enforced, that your child is fully involved with your funeral plans, that your choice of guardianship doesn't turn out to be regrettable, and that your child is adequately positioned for continued growth and development.

(a) *Putting Up Legal Protection*

The child with special needs is constantly in danger of being discriminated against, abused, or experiencing violence. This makes it very critical to provide them with the much-needed legal protection obtainable.

Statistics indicate that children with disabilities experience violence at levels that could be considered high — that is, in comparison to their peers without disabilities. Facts show that about 84 percent of children with disabilities report experiencing one form of violence or the other at school from one week to the next.

Also, children with disabilities are wrongly perceived and rated much less than other children by their abusers, making the latter view the former as easy targets for acts of violence and abuse as they (the differently abled or children with special needs) might be unable to flee, seek help, or be outspoken about their predicament, making them even more susceptible to further violence and abuse.

Even more challenging is the situation of the girl child with special needs or disabilities. This gender was typically more in the offing of experiencing and reporting emotional and sexual violence in comparison to their peers without disabilities. Studies did indicate that girls with disabilities (4 percent of girls surveyed) stood considerably more probable to experience sexual violence by school staff and report it compared to about 0.8 percent of girls without disabilities.

Further studies also indicate that children with disabilities find it challenging to get appropriate aid when they become victims of violence. This is because they lack requisite knowledge on where to go and whom to talk to, and even if they do know, they find it substantially tough to get there and effectively communicate with the child protection services staff. Some may even nurse concerns of not being taken seriously.

For instance, a parent might notice that their ward comes home with obvious traces of being bullied or beaten up. If the child is vocally impaired, it becomes increasingly challenging for them to voice their fears, concerns, and even name the perpetrators. This can further deepen the child's frustrations and elevate further concerns about their safety when outdoors.

Every parent desires to preserve the safety of their children, helping them lead healthier, happy lives. Comparatively, keeping children with special needs safe from harm and injuries is not at all different from keeping children without disabilities safe, to be candid. The challenge for parents with children having special needs, however, is accessing and assimilating information that pertains to the types of perils their children might be exposed to at different ages. Due to the uniqueness of individual children, general recommendations for effective safeguarding might not work for some due to their unique skills and abilities.

But as a responsible parent, you can begin to initiate steps that would ensure the safety of your child with special needs, no matter the level of disability they possess.

- Understand the challenges that young people with special needs go through in their schools, in their care environments, and workplaces.
- Understand what the laws say about protecting your child and young adults with special needs against stigmatizations, acts of violence, and discrimination.
- Understand your role in equipping your children with special needs to stand up for their rights where necessary.

(b) Prevailing Challenges Facing Children with Special Needs

The following are a few challenges that often confront children and young adults with special needs as they attempt to lead normal lives:

(i) Social exclusion

(ii) Abuse, maltreatment, and endangerment

(iii) Profiling and discrimination

(iv) Guardianship

(i) Social exclusion: It is important to realize that most societies have over the years formed biased dispositions toward the child with special needs, howbeit unintentionally. In the course of time, the outlook for any child with a disability or who has special needs has been from the viewpoint of their inabilities rather than from their strengths and abilities. This has led to the formulation of various forms

of exclusion, ranging from education and housing to responsibilities and opportunities.

Even though the right to various forms of social inclusion, like education for all, is widely accepted by many nations and emphasized in numerous treaties, children and young adults with special needs still do experience sharp exclusions, leading to their not getting the best from their society. Statistically, the rate of the pervasiveness of disability in the world's populations is currently 10–16 percent, with the number of children with disabilities presently in schools at a much lower rate. This shows that either a large number of children with special needs are not in school, or if they are, they remain unidentified.

In schools, for instance, the provision of educational and non-educational services conveyed in school surroundings are progressively identified as being essential to social inclusion, and it has also been proven to drastically reduce segregation.

Also, your child playing and having fun beyond their immediate familiar environment can be an essential participatory tool in their resident communities. Furthermore, the psychological well-being and physical health of your child might likely improve, as they engage in leisure and give their quota toward positive social interrelations.

Other things likely impact on the right to use and deliver inclusive services, which has been noted to affect young adults with special needs even more. Obstacles may consist of topographical challenges, which may or may not be man-made, the way public play equipment are designed and function, and housing complications. Other restrictions could include outlooks on parents and other associated adults and the absence of funding for services.

There are indications that some experts might have mixed feelings about effectively crafting play spaces, as access to conventional leisure amenities might be an important subject for many families.

(ii) Abuse, maltreatment, and endangerment: Vulnerable children have been plunged into dire circumstances in which they are forced, either due to economic reasons or by insensitive guardians, to work jobs for which they are not trained or old enough to do in order to survive. Child labor frequently takes place in tough conditions, which are generally hazardous, and contributes to educational impairment and increased vulnerability of the young child.

Statistically, it has been a challenge figuring out the precise ages and number of working children with special needs. But as far back as 2016, no less than 152 million children who were aged less than five worked; however, the figure is thought to be greatly undervalued due to the noninclusion of domestic labor.

Typically, abuse consists of misuse of power or an exercise of the same for unintended purposes. Child welfare systems do get involved when children, disabled or not, are caught up in the following situations:

1. *Physical abuse:* This involves assault or battery of the child with special needs. This might come about through the manipulation of the child to give consent to some form of extreme discipline or an outright physical action that the child never agreed to. Physical abuse can also border around irritation, provocation, and instigation of fear.
2. *Sexual abuse*: Sexual abuse ranges from direct to indirect assaults, consensual or nonconsensual intercourse, and other things like stalking and internet offenses.

3. **Neglect**: This is the failure to effectively safeguard a child from harm, and gross laxity in meeting the basic needs of the child with special needs. The safety of a child is strictly the responsibility of the parent or guardian, and if the child is abused in any way, then both the abusive and the negligent must be held responsible. In some cases though, they might be the same.
4. ***Psychological abuse***: Willfully providing what the child needs but with a blatant disregard for the feeling of the child is considered emotional abuse, which is a deliberate or inattentive instigation of emotional sorrow.

(c) Profiling and Discrimination

According to the United Nations reports, over ninety-three million children with disabilities worldwide are likely at risk of having their rights violated from the moment of being born. Furthermore, the reports suggest that millions of these children are separated from their families and retained in institutions where they are even more at risk of violence, mistreatment, and neglect.

Your child lives in a world where there are increased tendencies of being treated in particular ways that might be seen as unfair, discriminatory, and unacceptable. This can be avoided by understanding and teaching your child their rights in society. Also, there is a need to go further by providing them with a legal counsel who will stand to defend them within the ambit of the law if you are no longer in a position to do so in the future.

Here are a few rights that you must educate your wards about and see to it that they are defended even when you are not there to do so yourself:

(i) The right to air travel: All public airline companies are mandated by the Air Carrier Access Act to implement the necessary infrastructure that would accommodate people with special needs and physical disabilities, on the condition, however, that the carrier frequently attends to the general public. Facilities modifiable should take in priority seating, accessible airport facilities, and boarding assistance. Complaints about rights violations in this regard can be lodged with the U.S. Department of Transportation or a lawsuit in federal court.

(ii) The right to employment: Federal agencies/workspaces are mandated by the Rehabilitation Act to provide the adequate infrastructure that makes accessibility and work easier for people with disabilities. This act emphasizes the formulation of individualized plans for employment, which would be drafted for persons employed, even if such employees have special needs or disabilities.

Also, managers who have employees numbering up to at least fifteen persons are mandated to offer individuals with special needs or disabilities an equal opportunity to gain employment under ADA Title I. This is in pursuance of equal rights for people with special needs and disabilities as compared to other employees or applicants. For example, it would be unlawful for company recruiters to discriminate against an applicant for the reason that they are in a wheelchair. Similarly, employers are mandated not to inquire about the disability status of an applicant before making a job offer and must provide suitable accommodations to aid any known limitations of qualified applicants. Complaints about such discrimination are generally lodged with the U.S. Equal Employment Opportunity Commission.

Please note that proving discrimination in a court of law, especially when it has to employment can be extremely difficult. An employer who has to choose between ten applicants, for instance, might decide to pass on the individual with disabilities. When sued, the employer can refer to any reason why the candidate with disabilities was overlooked. In this situation, the suspicion of discrimination must be thoroughly examined by you and your attorney to help decide whether or not you have a case.

(iii) The right to education: The IDEA safeguards the rights of children with disabilities, such as visual or auditory impairments, to free and appropriate education. Typically, your child with special needs is expected to get an accessible education that is in equivalence with their peers, from age three to age twenty-one. It is unacceptable for physical disability or any special need to stop your child from learning along with their peer group. Following the six basic principles drawn in the IDEA, schools are mandated to:

- *Make public education that is free and appropriate available:* Schools must offer education at the expense of the public, all under the supervision and management of the public.
- *Carry out adequate evaluation:* It is mandatory for schools to collect relevant information that would help in determining the educational requirements of the child with special needs or disabilities. Furthermore, a guided decision-making procedure must be adopted for suitable educational programming.
- *Create a tailored education program:* Schools are mandated to fashion a written statement concerning tailored educational programs intended for children

with special needs. This would guarantee a total commitment to meeting the individual needs of the child.

- *Make available a learning environment of the least restriction:* The law enacts that children with special needs are authorized to get an education tailored appropriately to meet their needs. Separating children with special needs from their peers is done only if they cannot attain academic excellence within a general education classroom owing to the nature and extent of their disability, even alongside added aid and support.
- *Give room for active and evocative participation:* Schools are mandated to offer occasions for active and evocative participation throughout the special education process. This can also embrace the participation of parents and guardians.
- *Put in place routine precautions:* Routine precautions are meant to keep everyone within the boundaries of respecting the rights of parents and children with special needs or disabilities. It also puts in place a workable measure of resolving disputes and deadlocks. Furthermore, with routine precautions in place, parents can be part of sensitive school meetings; they can scrutinize any academic records and demand for a tailored educational evaluation.

(iv) The right to fair housing: Persons with disability are protected by the Fair Housing Act of 1968. It lets them buy or rent houses of their choice. The act compels homeowners and landlords to consider practical exceptions to housing policies so as to arrange for equal housing opportunities for people with special needs or disabilities. For instance, in home

apartments, where a "no pets" policy is maintained, landlords would have to make exceptions to the rule so as to accommodate a service dog for a tenant with visual impairment. Again, a landlord may have to consent to the modification of living space to allow for easy living for a family who cares for a child with special needs.

(v) The right to vote: Individuals with special needs and disabilities have their right to vote protected by the provision of physically accessible amenities required for effective voting under the Voting Accessibility for the Elderly and Handicapped Act. This would also include info delivered by teletype (TTY) and Telecommunications Device for the Deaf (TDD) to help individuals who are visually impaired.

(vi) The right to health care: The ADA mandates the implementation of communication tools for individuals with visual and auditory challenges within public spaces so as to accommodate their communication and navigation needs. For example, a person with a hearing impairment has the right to demand an interpreter who uses sign language when they go to visit the doctor.

(vii)The right to public transportation: Individuals with disabilities' right to access public transportation is protected under ADA Title II. The accessibility needs of individuals who use wheelchairs or those with hearing or visual loss must be accommodated on city buses and public rail transit. And in places where the use of public independent transportation is difficult, then the provision of paratransits must be considered.

If you feel the rights of your ward under any of these laws have been dishonored, you can do the following:

- Lodge in a complaint with the appropriate governing body overseeing the program. The U.S. Department

of Transportation, Aviation Consumer Protection Division, for instance, hears complaints regarding the Air Carrier Access Act.
- Make your concerns known to your special needs attorney who, in turn, can forward recommendations in line with relevant laws that would give you an upper hand upon pursuance within the school or in a court.
- Collect and keep records of the alleged discrimination. Make sure the records are thorough and verifiable, just in case you have to go to court to seek redress, and you are asked to provide the necessary proofs.

Alongside these aforementioned rights, you still need to have the following at the back of your mind:
- If your child's disability stands in the way of them getting gainful employment, you have to evoke their right to apply for Social Security Disability (SSD) and SSI; this would help with some extra income to handle various expenses. Even though SSD begins after a disability period of six months, SSI begins within a period of one month. However, qualification depends on your ward's passing the Disability Evaluation under Social Security.
- Get the services of a competent special needs attorney if you are disqualified from SSI and Disability. Your attorney can examine the details and help you overturn the denial.
- Disability-related prejudices and discrimination are firm grounds for litigation.
- Your disabled wards can be the victims of fraud. This is why the legal cover is always important. Once you

set up all that is required to protect them legally before you die, it becomes easier for their lawyers to defend and pursue justice for them if they ever fall prey to dupes and frauds.

Notable Points

(i) *It is important to put in place legal protection that would ensure the protection of your child's rights when you are no longer available to do so.*

(ii) *Challenges that often confront children/young adults with special needs include social exclusion, abuse, maltreatment, and endangerment, profiling and discrimination, and issues associated with guardianship.*

(iii) *Your child has the right to air travel, the right to employment, the right to education, the right to fair housing, the right to vote, the right to health care, and the right to public transportation.*

(iv) *There are various government agencies that would readily take up complaints of violations of any of these rights in defense of your ward.*

Actionable Steps

(i) *Write down any other areas where you feel your child's rights ought to be protected.*

(ii) *Research and find out other avenues of lodging complaints regarding rights abuses.*

― ― ―

Chapter 19
Guardianship

Guardianship is a legitimate proceeding in which a person asks the court to grant complete authority of their affairs to another to act as a guardian owing to the fact that the person can no longer manage their dealings effectively due to disability or in the event of their death. A guardian is then authorized to exercise such delegated authority on behalf of the person with disabilities or when the person dies.

On a general note, it can be quite tedious and expensive to initiate, manage, and effectively conclude the process of setting up a guardianship. This implies that it is not a process or decision that could be taken lightly.

Subject to the nature of a person's needs, guardianship can be categorized into two distinct kinds:

- *A person guardian:* This type of guardian is empowered by law to make pronouncements about an individual's food, clothing, housing, health care, and other subjects and issues that directly impact on the person.
- *A property guardian:* This type of guardian is empowered by law to only manage and make

pronouncements about an individual's funds, revenue, property, remunerations, and other financial matters.

(a) Pros and Cons of Guardianship

There are a number of reasons why guardianship can be of immense benefit to your adult child with special needs. First, guardianship would deal with some protection to your ward if they are noticeably at risk of being exploited and engaging in hazardous activities or conducts. The guardian would be empowered to make serious decisions concerning your child's place of residence, the kind of people they associate with, and be able to safeguard their funds and assets.

Guardianship would ensure the easiest means of getting things done is explored as they would deal directly with the beneficiary's banks, insurers, medical providers, phone companies, and others on behalf of your adult child.

The cons of this process also abound. First, it is likely that your adult child might not desire a guardian. And thanks to the requirement of the court for granting guardianship, you might be compelled to detail instances of your child's incompetence in decision-making. This is typically done in court, in the attendance of your child. Such an event may end up cutting deep wounds into your family bonds. Guardianship has been known to stir up disputes amongst households who may disagree on who should be the guardian and the amount of control to be seceded to the guardian over the life and affairs of the adult child.

Another downside of guardianship is the cost implication and the bureaucratic brouhaha that comes with it. A fee is paid at the instance of you asking the court for a guardianship, and you must present documentation of proof of your child's intellectual disability. Furthermore, the intended guardian might be compelled to submit themselves to a background check or even stake a bond if the child has possessions. Appointed guardians would be required to make ordered reports to the court.

Since the guardian is empowered by law to make all the decisions, the beneficiary under the guardianship doesn't get to exercise a great deal of freedom. Generally, guardianship is explored only if other less restrictive alternatives are not available as having special needs, physical, or mental challenges doesn't necessarily mean that one is incapable of making sound decisions.

There are a few alternatives to guardianship that you can explore. They could be implemented distinctly or in combination with one another if necessary to support the beneficiary to live as independently as possible.

- *(i)* ***Special needs trusts:*** For an adult with special needs, a special needs trust can serve the purpose as desired. We discussed this topic extensively in the last chapter and would encourage you to take a closer look at it once more.
- *(ii)* ***Family guidance:*** There might be no need for a guardian if a trusted family member is open to providing advice and care to your young child with special needs. On the other hand, if the person is easily compromised, then your child would be at risk of being taken advantage of, making guardianship the most appropriate option.
- *(iii)* ***Supported living services:*** If your ward only requires help in a few areas, then exploring programs, service providers, and professionals who can direct care in those distinct areas could be more beneficial. In

today's society, it is possible to get various types of services accessible to meet varying needs.

   (iv) Durable power of attorney: Your adult child, if competent enough, can go into a power of attorney agreement that exclusively names and empowers one specific individual, maybe a special needs attorney or a trusted relative, to make particular kinds of decisions on their behalf.

   (v) Financial representative: Here, you can set up representative payees or joint ownership for your child's bank accounts. This would help in the management of their finances.

(b) Naming a Guardian

Usually, states are more inclined to certain individuals to be named guardians. For wards with special needs who turn eighteen, the penchant is typically for parents. And if parents are not obtainable, then an adult sibling or family member would do. If no close relative or family is available, then a trusted family friend is appointed. The option of a professional guardian may suffice if the aforementioned options aren't obtainable.

A systematic tool for the prevention of any form of mismanagement of the beneficiary's finances, or taking any form of advantage of the same is done by subjecting the guardian to periodic court supervision. On occasion, particularly when dealing with professional guardians, the guardian is mandated to post a bond, which is a distinctive kind of insurance aimed at protecting the beneficiary's estate from mismanagement.

Also, guardians can be recompensed for their every expense, and in some cases, remunerated for their services. Usually, such payments come out of the assets they are taking care of and are made only to professional guardians, even though some states do allow a family member who has been appointed as guardian to pursue recompense in court.

In the event that the guardian cannot manage the estate, this does not automatically end the guardianship. Instead, a new guardian is chosen by the court. The guardian ought to think about who would be an ideal replacement, should he no longer be able to serve.

(c) The Determination of Competency

To grant guardianship, the judge must first determine the extent to which your young adult is unable to care for themself. Capacity is a molten concept that interweaves the individual, the conditions, and the decision to be made. This implies that the extent to which an individual can make a cognizant decision is directly linked to which decisions they are making, and a person can be capable of making some decisions, but not others.

To support the assertion that guardianship is necessary, an affidavit from your child's medical doctor confirming the level of aptitude, decision-making capability, prognosis, and diagnosis need be presented. Subject to state law, however, more proof might be required to establish the need for guardianship, proof from psychological evaluation, records of school performance, previous medical records, or individual testimonies.

By and large, sufficient evidence must be clear and substantial that your young child lacks the ability to make decisions and is unable to fare their property and affairs efficiently owing to their disability.

(d) Authorities and Obligations of the Guardian

Typically, the powers and onuses granted to the guardian would be clearly outlined by the court, and such would strictly be those needed in providing for the established needs of the child with special needs.

There are some cases where the guardian is obligated to seek distinct authorization from the court like in the case of a life-threatening medical treatment before such decisions are made. Furthermore, the guardian must file an annual report with the court. The report is meant to serve as a supervisory tool to checkmate the actions of the guardian, to confirm if the needs of the young adults with special needs are being satisfied, and to query whether or not there is any need for modifying or even terminating the guardianship. And as far as finances are concerned, the guardian is obligated to provide a record of everything achieved with the property beneath the guardianship order.

If a guardian flops in the performance of their duties as stipulated, then they risk removal or even litigation.

Notable Points

(i) *Guardianship is a legitimate process in which the court is asked to give complete authority of one's affairs to another, owing to the fact that the person can no longer manage their dealings effectively.*

(ii) *Guardianship is either person guardianship or property guardianship.*

(iii) *Other options to guardianship such as special needs trusts, family guidance, supported living services, power of attorney, and financial representative should first be explored, as guardianship can be quite precarious.*

(iv) *Before the court grants guardianship, the determination of competency must be carried out.*

(v) *Guardianship is a very serious responsibility. It can be revoked and claims made for damages.*

Actionable Steps

(i) Write down other viable options you are willing to explore apart from guardianship.

(ii) Write down potential guardians you might consider if it all came down to it.

(iii) Write down alternate names in the event that any of the guardians aren't available for the role.

(iv) Talk to your child, and tell them to hear their thoughts about it.

– – –

Chapter 20
Your Child with Special Needs and Their Workplace

Laws have been put in place by various states to help protect individuals with special needs or disabilities in the workplace. But due to some major adjustments made to the overall definition of disability by the Americans with Disabilities Act Amendments Act, employers have entertained questions as to how they are supposed to decide on whether or not an employee can be referred to as having a disability. These concerns typically come up when some extra levels of obligations, such as accommodation for the employee, are requested.

Going by the conventional definition of disability, which is a deficiency or impairment that largely restricts core life activity, employers need to understand the following:

- Does the employee have a deficiency or any form of impairment?
- In the case that the employee has, does the impairment impact core life activity?

- In the case that it does, does the impairment significantly hinder core life activity?

Employers need to consider the following when dealing with individuals with impairments of any kind:

- Think through what level of limitation the employee would have to endure if mitigations aren't put in place.
- Think through on the extent of the employee's limitation in the event the impairment is dynamic.
- Also think through the circumstance or period in which an employee accomplishes a core life activity.

As a parent, you are bound to be concerned about how your young child would do when they grow up, finish up from college, and attempt to lead normal lives. You would also fear how they would be treated in the workplace due to their disabilities and impairments, most especially when you think about the fact that you may not be there to see to their absorption, adaptation, safety, and the defending of their rights.

(a) Helping Your Child's Employer

If you are privileged to be around when your young child with special needs attempts to get employed, you can do your best to help them go through the process and clinch the job. Furthermore, you can help the employer the best way you can by doing the following:

- Help the employer know more about your child's special needs or disability beforehand. Help them set up where the young child would work, clearly outlining their duties and showing whom they would be working with. Ask that all equipment or machines that the young child would be working with is set up to accommodate their disability. For a youngster with visual impairment, you

should ensure that the employer installs Braille program on the computer, and if the youngster has a hearing impairment, you should ensure that the employer installs a screen reader app on their work computer.
- Inform your young child's employer about your child's limitations. Make a list of what they can and cannot do, while urging the employer to be sensitive to those needs.
- Insist that the employer makes much-needed provisions that would enable your child to do their job as best as they can, going by their ability.
- Inform your child's employer and, together, draft out a plan for days of meltdowns. Common with young individuals with autism, they may lose their cool in times of stress and anxiety. Tackling this challenge can be done by designating an area that the employee can go to find some "alone time" to calm down.
- Advise and see to it that a fellow employee is on standby to assist your young child having special needs, with imminent challenges or problems. You can encourage the employer to attach a staff that can help creatively manage the child's stress.
- Encourage your employer to include your child in all activities and howbeit after making a few adjustments where needed.
- You can insist that your child's remuneration should be commensurate to their level of work.
- Inform the employer that your child should be allowed to express themself whenever they want to.
- Ask for flexibility, patience, and empathy. Ask for multiple chances to correct behavior.

- Encourage employers to relate with your young child on their level of understanding. It is important not to treat them like children or people with low capacity for understanding.
- Encourage employers to use kind and appreciative words. This is important for boosting their self-esteem.
- Their employer should be encouraged to be respectful and yet firm. They should anticipate qualitative output and no excuses. Employers should treat youngsters with special needs like they would regular employees. It is important to discourage preferential treatment, except in certain situations. Nevertheless, it should be completely avoided.
- Encourage your child's employer to assume your child is as competent as the next employee within their strata. By assuming they are competent, their employer admits that they are able to do the job, knows what they are involved in, and is knowledgeable enough.

Here are a few things you should tell your child's employer that they should avoid:

- Encourage the employer never to exclude the youngster from any activity.
- Encourage the employer never to assume anything about your youngster, from them not understanding to them not wanting to participate.
- Encourage the employer never to engage in name-calling. Also, they should never ignore the young employee.
- Encourage the employer never to dismiss or fire your child with special needs for any expression associated with their disability. Always make room for them to express themselves so everyone can work together in harmony.

- Encourage the employer to never work with your child having special needs, based on assumptions. They should always ask consent first, particularly when it comes to physical contact with the child, moving their work tools or personal effects.

It is important to understand the task your child is getting into. Also, you have to be knowledgeable of the relevant laws that concern the employment of individuals with disabilities.

(b) Helping Your Child Meet up and Speak Up

It is imperative that you educate your young adult with special needs on what to expect and how to behave at their workplace. This knowledge would help them meet up with expected demand from their employers and speak up when they feel uncomfortable or are being harassed.

- Encourage them to put in their best. Let the young adult know that work means responsibility and ought to be taken very seriously.
- Encourage them to be respectful of their bosses and coworkers. Your child must understand that respect is a commodity that must be given and earned.
- Encourage them to be bold and confident. No employer wants an employee around who is timid and can hardly function due to low self-esteem.
- Encourage them to speak on any concerns they may have. Your child must be made to realize that asking for more clarification on an assignment, asking to take a break, or asking for help is normal and should be done.
- Encourage them to stand up for their rights. Your child must learn assertiveness, not allowing their rights to be abused without saying a word.

- Encourage them to be open. Your child should be told to open up to their employer over any concerns that they may have.

Notable Points
(i) The rights of your child must be respected in their workplace.
(ii) There are enacted laws that protect your child from abuse and discrimination in the workplace.
(iii) A mutual understanding between you, the caregiver, and the employer can help smooth things for your young adult.
(iv) Furnish your ward's employer with relevant information about your child and their disabilities.
(v) Encourage your child to be responsible while still looking out to stand up for their rights if need be.

Actionable Steps
(i) Write down ideas that could help foster a cordial relationship with your child's employer.
(ii) Write down creative ways that could help employers effectively communicate and respect the right of your child.

Write down ideas on how to communicate responsibly to your child.

– – –

Chapter 21
Your Child's Involvement in Your Funeral Plans

It is no mistake that most parents love their children dearly and want to do whatever needs to be done to protect them from the tough aspects of life. But appreciating the fact that a funeral serves as both a rite of passage and a vital aspect of the grieving process is a key lesson to learn. The decision to involve your child with special needs when preparing your funeral is entirely up to you. For a lot of children, being a part of the planning process and the eventual attendance of the funeral truly does help them in moving forward in their grieving process.

Just like grown-ups, children do need a chance to bid their goodbyes, so placing the choices before them and helping them prepare beforehand are important factors to consider.

Before being allowed to make such a decision, it is important that you take time out to expound on the subject. If they have never attended or been involved in the planning of a funeral, they would hardly know how it is done or its purpose. Simplifying the description and explanations can be very helpful in making the young child decide on whether or not to be part of the planning and whether or not to even attend it when the time comes. It is also imperative to keep the conversation age appropriate and endeavor to employ words that won't scare off the child.

(a) Guidelines for Assisting Children through a Funeral

Your child might likely choose to attend your impending funeral, and it's essential to ensure that you provide the support they require before the time. Remember, this might also be a completely new experience for them. In the way you were careful to make their first day of school as seamless as possible, you have to apply the same wisdom for a funeral. Have a conversation about the subject with them, and help them realize what to expect.

(b) Get Them Ready before It Happens

The art of surprise might be counterproductive, most especially on a sensitive subject such as death and funerals. Most adults would prefer to have the foreknowledge of an event, so they can be better prepared, how much more children. Explain the process to your child with special needs, step by step. Discuss what your child might likely see; things like seats, sacred symbols, florae, casket, vases, the body of the departed, black clothing, and so on. Let the conversation be systematic and effective. The idea is to educate and familiarize the child with what to expect, so do not try to exhaust the subject in one sitting. Instead, allow the conversation to sink in day by day, approaching it in small measures. Eliminate any anxiety from your child, and help them prepare for a new experience.

(c) Illuminate Them on What Death Is

As much as people have come to associate death with something bad or not worth ever experiencing, it is important that you give your child a healthy perspective about the subject. You must make it clear that death is inevitable and must be seen as a part of life, even though it comes with grief and sorrow. You must strive to be the conveyor of such information, not relying on third parties who might present distorted views to your child. Furthermore, you must be sensitive to the age and maturity level of your child with special needs when trying to have this conversation, as young children not more than seven years of age would prefer basic concept explanations, whereas older children are more capable of understanding more complex explanations. But expectantly, your goal should be to help them come to terms with the physicality of death and how the body seizes to function upon one's demise. You may choose to go along with your religious beliefs, explaining what may happen to the soul of the dead. But this is subject to what you and your family holds as sacred. Be clear and guileless, employing the words *"dead"* along with its other variations as often as possible. Do not use euphemisms; this might mislead your child to see death as something not as serious as it is.

(d) Let Them Know Having Feelings Is OK

Make it clear to your child with special needs that funerals come with experiencing emotions, both from themselves and the people around them at the event. It is also important to point out that these emotions may be sad and sober, but are necessary for going through a transition. Point out that many people will be sad, and that it is natural to feel that way after someone dies. Also, explain that emotions might differ from person to person, and from event to event. Simply because a person isn't crying doesn't mean they aren't feeling the weight of the demise, and people may generally be sober at the funeral service, but later be jolly at the reception. Explain it clearly to your child that all these are normal.

(e) Pay Attention to Their Needs

Take note of how your child reacts to the discussion, and inquire about their feelings. Children process such information in different ways, depending on their level of maturity. Do not ignore it when the conversation becomes intense. Allow for breaks or periods of relief. You can take them for a walk and help them catch their breath. Allow them to process the information at their own pace. Still, do not underestimate them; they may astonish you with how well they might handle it all.

(f) Have Time to Answer Their Questions

Your child with special needs might have a few questions and concerns regarding the subject. It is important that you respond to them one after the other. Let your answers and responses be as simple and honest as they can be, with no element of shaming. Each response might help them come to terms with the imminent event and correct any wrong notion that they might have. The questions will vary from simple and straightforward to complicated and complex. Admit to your child that you do not know all the answers and are willing to help them understand. This would help them be patient with answers.

(g) How to Involve Your Child with Special Needs in Funeral Planning and Funeral Service

Involving your child in the planning and arrangement of your funeral can serve as a subtle tool in helping them make peace with the event even before it happens. It would also help them further understand bereavement, sorrow, and the importance of honoring the lives of people before they die. Funeral directors should work with you and your child with special needs, taking into cognizance the age of your ward and finding age-appropriate methods for them that would encourage participation.

(h) Involving Children in Funeral Planning

Typically, a funeral plan would capture the various aspects of the event that only professionals could put together from start to finish. However, there can be room for other areas of the event to be spiced up by specifically tailored activities and arrangements that might interest your child with special needs. Their contribution to such areas could give them a sense of participation. Here are a few simple, yet evocative ways your child can be involved, adding in some personalization:

- Gather photographs of their cherished moments with you and create a *tribute video*. Assist them in sifting through the family's old photo albums, engaging them in discussions that would spur their memories to recollect moments that they might regard as precious. Avoid triggering sober emotions as this might be counterproductive, causing the child to shut down.

- You can help your child with special needs come up with and decorate memorial displays about you and other loved ones. Also, your child can help organize beautifications on the memorial display; this would help create a tailored tribute to proudly showcase at the funeral.

- Collaborate with them in the choice of songs, poems, special readings, prayers, or speech marks to be used in the funeral ceremony. Emphasize to them that their choices would mean the world to you and ought to be taken seriously.

- Encourage them to write notes or letters or even make art drawings that would be placed within the casket. This would give them a sense of eternal closeness to you even after you pass away. Their choice of what to put within the casket shouldn't be limited to writing or drawings; instead, let them come up with something creative, which they see as special. Nevertheless, it shouldn't be bulky or too much to be placed in the casket.
- Your child should be encouraged to help in the selection of the postfuneral reception meals. Involving them in the postfuneral planning can also help them become increasingly comfortable before, during, and after the funeral.

(i) Involvement in Funeral Services

There are a lot of ways to include a child during the funeral service. Regardless of whether or not they are at ease with public speaking, they can be involved with other things that could be regarded as more behind-the-scenes, such as:

- Your child could be chosen to be the candle bearer or even be the one to light the candle. This, however, is subject to your family beliefs and religious practices.
- Your child could be asked to read a poem, perform a song, or do a presentation during the funeral service. If they are not comfortable doing such acts alone, you can suggest they do it along with a friend or in groups. This would make them feel more at home.
- Your child can be given the role of helping set up memorial displays for the funeral service. They could also be asked, alongside some of their peers, to help organize the funeral flowers and any sympathetic flowers delivered by visiting mourners to the funeral service. They could also be engaged in the disposal of the flowers to local hospitals or hospice centers after the service.

- Your child could be encouraged to share memories aloud with guests or create a memory box where thoughts and prayers would be dropped at the funeral service.
- Your child can play the role of a greeter at the visitation. This simply means that they would greet arriving guests at the funeral visitation, showing them where to sign the funeral register book and other relevant information.

Funerals can be extremely tiring. It is recommended that a separate room be set aside during the funeral service. With this, your child can find a space to rest and take some time away from the funeral activities

Notable Points

(i) *You can help your child prepare for what is imminent by talking with them about the subject.*

(ii) *Take the time to explain to them what death is, that having and expressing their feelings is OK.*

(iii) *Do not ignore their needs, but set aside time to answer their questions.*

(iv) *You can request that the funeral director involves your child in the planning of the event.*

(v) *You can request that your child be allowed to play certain roles at the event.*

(vi) *You can help your child begin the process of transiting even before you die.*

Actionable Steps

(i) *Take out time to plan the event with your child.*

(ii) *Research on roles that they can play in the event.*

(iii) *Plan to help them make peace with the event even before it comes.*

Chapter 22
Securing Continued Growth and Development

One of the many questions that has to be asked is, "Is the development of the child on track?" This question is critical as parents, educators, pediatricians, and caregivers look to see if all efforts meted out to the child are yielding desired growth and change.

In a bid to adequately respond to this important question, child development specialists have crafted diverse amounts of checklists and charts that would assist you in keeping track of your child's development across a number of key domains:

- corporal development
- intellectual development
- linguistic development
- social-emotional development

It is important to note that there might be variations between the lists. Each checklist might evaluate a set of items, but it isn't exhaustive in itself. So your evaluation might be very limited if you go by only the responses in this checklist. Research indicates that this checklist houses about forty developmental milestones, whereas there are seven hundred and twenty eight milestones that could be used to evaluate your child. This, then, begs the question of whether or not you should rely on a single checklist.

Researchers recommend starting with having a parent-pediatrician conversation. This is important as the yardsticks employed by doctors may be poles apart from those typically being used by parents. Furthermore, your child's health care provider may screen your child for any developmental delays via authenticated screening tools.

Additionally, to appreciate your child's continued development, it would be helpful to think of development as being an individual progression, rather than simply a list of boxes to tick at suggested breaks. Once a noticeable pause is seen in your child's progress, then you might need to speak with your child's health care provider. And identifying a delay early can be the difference between salvaging the situation and letting it go bad altogether.

(a) Developmental Milestones

Milestones are best described as the things a child ought to be able to do by a certain age. Typically, children of the same age range do develop skills and abilities in approximately the same sequence; however, the timeframes might differ sometimes. This variance goes from one child to the other, in the same fashion as hair and eye colors do. So every child grows and develops at a pace that can best be termed as individualistic. Let us take a closer look at some common milestones ascribed to each age period.

(i) Tools for developmental reviews

1. *From birth to eighteen months:* The growth of a baby during this period is profound, and the changes are rapid. Medical professionals do recommend that you consciously speak to your baby during this phase, as it would assist in the development of their communication skills. Other recommendations include:

- Short phases of tummy time to help in the strengthening of the neck and back muscles of your baby. Ensure, however, that the baby is awake and that you are close by.
- Give quick responses to your baby's cries. Pick up and comfort; this would build a strong bond between you and the baby.

Birth to Eighteen Months Development Table

	Reasoning	*Social And Emotive*	*Verbal*	*Movement/ Corporal*
1–3 Months	Displays curiosity in objects, human faces, moving things, etc. May be uninterested in repetitive activities.	Attempts at looking at your face or that of others. Begins to grin.	Starts to make vocal sounds, like cooing. Begins to respond to your vocal sounds, like becoming calm when you speak to them. Yelps in different ways, depending on the needs.	Motions toward the direction of the sounds. Trails moving objects with eyes. Clutches objects firmly. Increasingly raises head for extended periods.

4–6 Months	Distinguishes acquainted faces. Recognizes music. Reacts to gestures of love and affection.	Reacts to facial lexes. Relishes frolicking with others. Reacts distinctly to dissimilar voice tones.	Starts to hubbub or mimic sounds. Begins to laugh.	Sees items and stretches out to grab them. Uses arms to push upward when lying on tummy. May attempt to roll over.
5–9 Months	Takes hands up to mouth. Moves items from one hand to the other.	Relishes mirrors. Recognizes when an unfamiliar person is around.	Reacts to the calling of their name. Begins to add consonant sounds. Begins to communicate using gestures.	Begins to sit up without any help. Might bounce when held up standing. Begins to roll in both directions.

9–12 Months	Looks intently at items as they fall. Begins to seek for hidden things.	Becomes figure-hugging and may have strong preference for accustomed people.	Begins to point finger. Recognize the meaning of certain words, like "no." Mimics sounds and motions.	Begins to pull up to standing position. Crawls.
12–18 Months	Learned how to hold and use some basic items, like spoons. Can identify named body parts by pointing.	Can participate in simple imaginary games. May employ outbursts. Would cry around an unfamiliar person.	Knows how to say several words. Says "no." Waves bye-bye.	Walks holding onto surfaces. Stands alone. May climb a step or two. May drink from a cup.

2. **Eighteen months to two years:** This period of development will comprise plenty of sleep, healthy nutrition, and building kindred relationships with you, the parent, and other caregivers. Here are a few pieces of advice for developing a safe space aimed at maximizing the early development of your child:

- Draft out a foreseeable routine on which to keep your child. This would leave them feeling safe and grounded.
- Make your house and play area toddler proof. This is to avoid accidents and injuries.
- Employ gentle discipline in guiding and teaching your child. Shun smacking, which can likely bring about the physical and emotional injury in the long run.
- Engage in activities that can help boost your child's vocabulary, such as singing, talking, and reading to them.
- Observe your child for indications about the dependability of other caregivers.
- Do not focus on your child to the point of ignoring your health. Your child needs you to be healthy.

Eighteen Months to Two Years Development Table

	Reasoning	Social and Emotive	Verbal	Movement/ Corporal
18 months	Begins to recognize familiar items in picture form. Recognizes what familiar objects do. Scribbles on	Begins to assist with tasks, like packing toys. Feels proud of accomplishments. Identifies self in mirror. Likely to	Recognizes a number of words. Follows the simplest of directions. Enjoys short stories and songs.	May attempt to get dressed. Starts to run. Can drink comfortably from

	paper or surfaces. Adheres to singular requests.	start exploring environs.		a cup. Can eat with a spoon. Can move around while still pulling a toy.
24 months	Can build Lego towers. Begins to follow two-part directives. Can group similar shapes and colors. Can play imaginary games.	Appreciates play dates. Can play alongside other children. May even begin to play with them. May seek to explore defying directives, such as "come back here."	Begins to ask simple questions. Begins to name familiar items. Begins to use simple two-word phrases for communication. Utters the names of accustomed people.	Can run. Can jump. Can stand on tiptoes. Begins to draw lines and shapes. Can throw balls and objects. Might attempt to climb stairs using rails.

3. Three to five years: This is a period that sees your child getting increasingly independent and clever. This age is typically when the child gets into preschool. Here, they experience a surge in curiosity, as those around them begin to expand. The formation of new friendships, new experiences, and new environments begins to impact their outlook.

Here are a few recommendations for this period:

- Sustain an ardent reading culture for your child.
- Use illustrations to exemplify responsibility at home.
- Be deliberate, clear, and unfailing with your anticipations. Take the time to explain what conducts you desire from your child.
- Relate with your child using age-appropriate language.
- Assist your child in solving problems when they are on emotional rollercoasters.
- Keep an eye out for your child when playing in outdoor spaces.
- Support your child's choices about how to interrelate with other household members and unfamiliar persons.

Three To Five Years Development Table

	Reasoning	Social And Emotive	Verbal	Movement/ Corporal
3 years	Is able to put a 3–4 part puzzle together. Is able to play	Displays empathy. Gives affection. Recognizes	Is able to communicate using two or more sentences. Can	Is able to walk up and down the steps with one foot on each tread.

	with toys that have moving parts. Is able to manipulate door knobs. Is able to flip through book pages.	simple yet distinct word differences, like "mine" and "yours." Can be too attached to routines. Is able to get dressed.	comfortably name items used daily. Is able to speak and be understood, most especially by family.	Can easily run and jump. Is able to catch a ball. Is able to play sliding down a slide.
4 years	Should begin to count. Is able to draw stick figures. Might be able to predict outcomes of tales and stories. Is able to participate in a simple board game.	Might be able to understand role-playing games with roles like "father" and "baby." Plays with other kids. Is able to communicate likes and dislikes. May pretend to a fault; might have challenge distinguishing	Is able to recall daily activities. Communicates in sentences. May identify or use rhymes. Is able to pronounce first and last name.	Can hammer a peg into a hole. Walks backward. Climbs stairs confidently. Can hop. Pours liquids with some help.

	Is able to identify a few colors, numbers, and capital letters.	between real and pretend.		
5 years	Is able to draw more complex figures. Is able to count up to ten items. Is able to craft out simple shapes. Can grasp simple processes. Is able to mention names.	Able to differentiate gender. Enjoys playing with friends. Is able to sing, dance, and may play act. Interchanges from being obedient and being disobedient. Can't differentiate between real and unreal.	Is able to tell stories, even staying on track. Is able to recite nursery rhymes. Is able to name letters and numbers. Is able to answer simple questions, mostly about stories.	May be able to somersault. Uses scissors. Hops or stands on one foot for about ten seconds. Can swing on swing set Goes to the bathroom in the toilet.

4. *School-age development*: At this period, the child experiences rapid growth in the areas of independence and competence. Furthermore, the child forms a high tolerance for friends and their influence on them. Also, the self-confidence of the child would be grossly impacted by academic and social challenges that abound within the learning environment.

As a parent at this stage, your challenge would be to find a balance between maintaining their safety, enforcing discipline, sustaining family interconnectivity, giving room for some level of decision-making and inspiring them to embrace growing responsibility. Regardless of this speedy growth, children at this stage still need parents to set boundaries and embolden healthy habits.

Here are a few tips to apply:
- Ensure they rest a great deal.
- Encourage them to be active in sports and to perform regular exercise.
- Make a quiet reading space, filled with positivity for home study.
- Put a cap on screen time, monitoring online activities as much as you can.
- Cultivate healthy, positive family traditions.
- Communicate the subject of consent and set corporal boundaries.

School-Age Development Table

	Reasoning	Social And Emotive	Verbal	Movement/ Corporal
6–8 years	Can complete directives of three or more steps. Can count in reverse.	Collaborates with others. May have fun playing with kids of dissimilar genders.	Can read grade-level books. Understands speech.	Can jump rope. Can do art or painting. Can complete

	Knows left and right. Can read a clock.	Imitates adult manners. Feels jealous. May be shy about body parts.		basic grooming tasks, like brushing of teeth, combing of hair. Can practice physical skills.
9-11 years	Can manipulate common devices, such as smartphones and game consoles. Writes comprehensive stories and letters. Can sustain attention for a longer period.	May have a close or best friend. Can reason from another person's perspective. Experiences more pressure from peers.	Listens with intent for catching reasons, such as pleasure or learning. Forms basic opinions from hearing. Can follow instructions on paper. Draws rational conclusions from reading. Can compose based on a	May begin to see signs of early puberty. Pubic hair growth, breast development. Amplified skill levels in sports and corporal activities.

			stated idea Can plot and give a discourse.	
12-14 years	Advances outlooks and opinions that may be different from that of parents. Becomes aware that parents aren't always right. Can comprehend metaphorical semantics. Increased ability to think logically, howbeit still very tender.	May become more self-governing from parents. Displays more irritability. Seeks more room for privacy.	Can use speech that isn't literal. Can employ voice tonality when communicating intentions; may use sarcasm.	Many females will have started periods. Advances on minor sex features, such as armpit hair, changes in voice. Changes in height or weight. This would be quick, then may slow down.

| 15–17 years | Assume habits for work and study. Can elucidate their opinions and adoptions. Continued divergence from parents | Amplified curiosity in courting and sexual relations. Devotes more time with friends compared to family. Continued growth in empathy toward others. | Fluent in speaking, reading, listening, and writing. Can have multifaceted discussions. Can speak adaptively to different groups. Can write convincingly. Can comprehend maxims, metaphoric language, and analogies. | Continued physical maturity. |

5. *When you have concerns:* There is a distinct possibility that you may nurse concerns about the general development of your child. And when dealing with a child with special needs, where such developments might not be as rapid and up to par as expected, still, there ought to be some progress, which would give you concern if not seen over time. Nevertheless, you can explore a few options available to you.

First, have a chat with your child's pediatrician, requesting for a developmental screening. It is common knowledge that the screening tools adopted by doctors are more detailed and thorough compared to downloadable online checklists and, thus, might give you more dependable information on the abilities and progress being made by your child.

If you still feel unsatisfied, you can go on to request a referral from your pediatrician to go visit a developmental specialist for further analysis. Specialists like an occupational therapist, pediatric neurologist, or a psychologist who specializes in evaluating children, or a speech/language therapist can all run various assessments to determine your child's progress.

You can communicate with the special education director of the public school closest to your home if your child is three years old or older. It doesn't matter if your child is registered at that school or not; you can always ask for a developmental evaluation. Be sure to pen down dates and relevant names for follow up where necessary.

There is no reason to delay if you suspect a developmental delay because a lot of developmental problems can be tackled more efficiently once there is early intervention.

Child development is systematic and can be tracked. Babies, kids, and school-age children cultivate new abilities in a stable progression as they age. Even though this can be tracked on a general note, it is important to note that every child develops at a distinct pace. The use of developmental milestone checklists can assist in enlightening parents and caregivers who desire to find out if their child is growing as expected.

If you nurse a concern about the likelihood of a neglected milestone, your pediatrician can have a discussion with you to carry out a developmental screening so as to get a clearer picture. You can also choose to link up with developmental specialists, special education, and early intervention programs in local schools to have an evaluation done.

Robust parent-child connections, healthy nutrition, enough rest, and a secure, nurturing home and school environment can help guarantee that children have the finest chance of developing as they ought to.

Notable Points

(i) *The evaluation of child development is typically viewed across these key domains, which are corporal development, intellectual development, linguistic development, and social-emotional development.*

(ii) *Tools for developmental are typically reviewed from birth to eighteen months, eighteen months to two years, three to five years, and school-age development levels.*

(iii) *It is expected that children at these levels would show some behavioral traits.*

(iv) *If you suspect that there are some delays in your child's overall growth, it is important to speak with a specialist.*

Actionable Steps

(i) *Study the charts provided.*

(ii) *Mark the level that your child falls into, and evaluate their progress.*

(iii) *Talk with a professional to determine any delays in growth.*

(iv) *Enroll in an assessment from your child's pediatrician.*

Conclusion

The idea of exiting the scene without making adequate preparation for the welfare of your child with special needs is unimaginable. It is a well-known fact that most parents live to simply give the best to their kids. This implies that no matter what they acquire, it would all mean nothing if it cannot meet the immediate and future needs of their wards when they are no more.

The fear of leaving them all alone in a vulnerable world should spur us to explore various ways that we can help secure their future. Preparing them for the inevitable is always the first step to take. If you take the time to have the conversation about death with your child, it would be easier for them to transition from grieving and mourning to living normally after the event occurs.

We cannot deny that the death of a loved one might be extremely devastating to any child. This further buttresses the fact that an early discussion about the subject and a deliberate attempt at preparing them for such a loss can mitigate any form of shock that would shake them to the core. Children are great at adapting and could make peace with the subject even before it occurs.

Again, putting necessary steps in place should follow. You must face the fact that you owe them personal care and healthy bonding. Their living spaces ought to be adequately nurtured to help them grow and develop as they ought to. Furthermore, their interactions with society should also spur them to happier and healthier living.

Their education must be taken seriously, as well. You have to explore various platforms that could offer them seamless, top-of-the-notch special education, tailored specifically for them. Again, explore options set up by the government geared at making the lives of children with special needs and disabilities worthwhile. There a number of academic and social supports that you could explore that would help you manage your child's challenges more efficiently without drilling a hole through your finances.

The health care of your child is paramount but can be extremely expensive. By taking advantage of the many aids and supports given by governments and many nonprofit organizations, you open your child to a variety of assistance.

The need for legal coverage is something you ought to take seriously. Dying without any form of estate planning can be counterproductive to your family, especially to your child with special needs. Your child needs the law to secure whatever assets you bequeath to them, no matter how small. Write a will to help avoid putting your family through the hassle of having to rely on the courts to determine who gets what from your estate when you are dead. Also, setting up other tailored documents, like a special needs trust, can assist your child in securing their inheritance to a time when they are fully mature to manage it, or if that isn't obtainable, in the hands of a trusted guardian, who would manage their affairs on their behalf.

The law is there to guide and protect the interests of your child with special needs all the way. You need to use all available legal tools to secure the future of your ward. Other conduits exist by which you can secure assets for your ward. You can explore life insurance policies, draft an LOI, and so on. All these are tailored toward helping you achieve your wishes for your child after you die.

The choice of a guardian would also have to tackled, as any aberration on the subject could mean relying on the courts to give such authority to whomever they deem fit to hold it. It is important to name a guardian for your child with special needs so that you can rest assured that your wishes and desires regarding your estate and your child are carried out in detail.

It would mean the world if they were left to fend in an environment that is friendly, respectful, and encouraging. Despite the amount of abuse, neglect, and treachery being experienced in the world today, you can put mechanisms in place that can help your child live a normal life long after you are gone. One of the vital things to do is to schedule occasional routine evaluations to ascertain the level of progress and development your child has experienced in the last few years. This exercise will help you track areas where your child might be experiencing delays and areas that you need to put in extra in order to help your child.

Helping your child when they are ready for the workplace is equally important. You can work alongside their employer to help them settle in and work like any other competent worker employed. Furthermore, you can talk with the employer to consider a few things to do to help your child make the most of the opportunity. It is imperative to encourage the employer to apply a lot of patience, understanding and empathy, without necessarily compromising competence and responsibility.

In trying to secure the future for your child, it is important to remember that your child's most cherished memories of you would be those spent together. Do not underestimate the impact you may be having on your child while you are alive. Their lives would never be the same without you, but be sure to give them your time, effort, and love, so that when you are gone, they would have something to hold on to that money cannot buy. Do not be tempted to simply store up as many treasures as you might for them without giving them what matters the most, which is yourself.

The bond formed by you and other members of your household would be the most important lifeline, which your child would hold on to when the time of mourning comes. Allow them to have the best of you while you are still here. The fear of imminent neglect should not be allowed to drive you away from your child with special needs, but to motivate you to be closer than ever before.

– – –

Printed in Great Britain
by Amazon